THE NEW GROLIER ENCYCLOPEDIA OF
WORLD WAR II

THE NEW GROLIER ENCYCLOPEDIA OF

WORLD WAR II

THE EASTERN FRONT

Grolier Educational Corporation
Sherman Turnpike, Danbury, Connecticut 06816

GROLIER EDUCATIONAL CORPORATION

Editorial
Remmel Nunn, *Vice President and Publisher*
Molly Stratton, *Editor, New Reference Titles*
Marge Heckler, *Administration*

Sales
Robert R. Hall, *Senior Vice President, Sales*
Robert Buck, *Regional Vice President, Sales*
Vincent J. Lamenza, *Regional Vice President, Sales*
Vern Nepple, Regional *Vice President, Sales*
Larry Tinker, Regional *Vice President, Sales*
Christine Lawlor, *Sales Analyst*
Donna Mikolajczyk, *Administration*

Marketing
Beverly A. Balaz, *Vice President, Marketing*
Mark Zielinski, *Director of Marketing*
Kathleen Santini, *Marketing Services Coordinator*
Charlene Hines-Gailliard, *Telemarketing Team Leader*
R. Scott Brown, *Telemarketing Training Specialist*
Jennifer Rux, *Exhibits and Administration*

Operations
Laraine Balk Hope, *Vice President, Operations*
Cynthia Gerrish, *Operations Administrator*

Finance
Mary Kay Doty, *Controller*
Susan Foote, *Accountant*

This library edition first published 1995 by Grolier Educational Corporation.
Copyright © 1995 Marshall Cavendish.

ISBN 0-7172-7508-6

Cataloging information and catalog card kits are provided separately
at no extra charge.

•

Editorial staff
Editors: Tim Cooke, Susie Dawson
Senior Designer: Wayne Humphries
Designer: Ricky Newport
Text: Paul Rodgers, Sarah Halliwell
Index prepared by Indexing Specialists, Hove, England
Printed in Singapore by Imago

CONTENTS

THE EASTERN FRONT

THE EASTERN FRONT

In the mind of Adolf Hitler, Nazi dictator of Germany, the greatest obstacle to realizing his dream of a Reich, or empire, which would dominate Europe lay to the east: The vast Soviet Union. In 1917 Russia, as the Soviet Union was then known, had been rocked by revolution which overthrew the monarchy and established in its place the Bolshevik Party, who established a communist nation where all power, property, and business were concentrated in the hands of the state.

Joseph Stalin, Soviet leader since 1924, planned to reinforce communism in his own country, before taking the revolution abroad. Under his modernizing schemes, the economy improved greatly, but his people suffered as their leader forced many of them into slave labor, and executed millions more.

Meanwhile, Hitler was highly suspicious of Stalin. The German had long hated communism, and blamed communists – among others such as Jews – for the dire economic and social situation in which Germany found herself after World War I. Although he had signed a pact with Stalin in which both promised not to attack the other's country, Hitler still saw Russia's massive resources as a critical part of his master plan: He could claim its vast lands and use its citizens for labor.

In June 1941 Hitler's troops invaded the Soviet Union in Operation Barbarossa, a lightning three-pronged thrust designed to drive to the heart of the Soviet empire – Moscow. Despite its vast size, the Soviet Red Army was handicapped by inferior, out-dated equipment and poor leadership: Stalin had executed many of his best generals. For a while it seemed as though Hitler's plan would succeed. Within five months, fast-moving panzer tank divisions had raced across the vast steppes – or plains – of central Russia to come within 20 miles of the center of Moscow. Meanwhile, in the north, troops were besieging Leningrad, now called St. Petersburg, on the shores of the icy Baltic Sea; to the south they drove toward the Crimea Peninsula on the Black Sea. But the German advance had finally run out of steam: Operation Barbarossa had failed.

For the next four years, the German troops would fight their weary way back to their homeland, pursued by the reinvigorated Red Army. In part, they had been defeated by the sheer size of the Soviet Union, and in part by the determination with which the Soviet people defended their country. But they had not anticipated their most powerful enemy – the fierce Russian winter. The freezing weather would return each year as the Red Army drove them relentlessly out of Russia, across Eastern Europe, and ultimately back into Germany and the heart of the Reich.

There, from his underground bunker in the center of Berlin, Hitler still insisted that victory was possible. Only when Russian troops were fighting in the streets around him did he accept that his dream was dead and commit suicide. Shortly afterward, the city fell to the Red Army and the war in Europe came to an end.

But if the threat of Nazism was dead, the end of the war brought a new instability to the world. The advance toward Berlin had left Russian troops in control of the occupied countries of Eastern Europe – Poland, Czechoslovakia, Romania, and the nations of the Balkan Peninsula. After the war, many of these countries became communist, helping the Soviet Union become one of the world's two greatest superpowers. The unity the Allies had shared during the war was soon forgotten as the Soviet Union on one hand and the US on the other launched the Cold War, the long period of hostility and tension between the two that would dominate world politics for some 50 years.

BARBAROSSA

Hitler had made a nonagression pact with Joseph Stalin, dictator of the Soviet Union. But in June 1941, driven by his hatred of communism, Hitler turned on his ally. It was a military gamble which would cost him dear.

Silhouetted against a burning village, a Soviet T34 tank advances, ready for battle (below). Until the production of the T34 late in 1940, Russian tanks were no match for the powerful German panzers.

For the young Adolf Hitler, serving as a corporal in the German army during the First World War, the tales told by the veterans returning from the fight against Russia on the Eastern Front were more than simply stories. They would have a lasting effect, not only on the young man, but on the whole of Germany and Russia. Their accounts of the overthrow of the Russian czar in 1917 by the Bolsheviks – communist revolutionaries led by Lenin – fueled Hitler's hatred of the new Soviet government's philosophy and his

belief that the Russian people were *Untermenschen*, or subhumans. His hatred endured and grew: Amid the poverty and turmoil that gripped Germany after the harsh Versailles peace treaty which brought World War I to an end, Hitler's Nazi Party led violent demonstrations against the communists, whom they blamed for the country's problems. Over long years, as his political power increased, it became Hitler's quest to destroy communism. Finally, in June 1941, now dictator of Germany, he ordered the launch of Operation Barbarossa – the German invasion of the Soviet Union. The decision would have repercussions on the war throughout Europe and North Africa.

The commander of the South Western Front, Marshal Budenny (right), a prewar friend of Stalin, owed his position more to influence than skill, and his command was virtually wiped out as the Germans advanced. The hatband insignia of a Soviet army general (left).

Before dawn on June 22, a party of Brandenburgers – elite German troops – slipped across the Polish border wearing the drab brown uniforms of Russian infantrymen for disguise. Their goal was the capture of bridges across the rivers Niemen, Bug and Prut, vital for the main German invasion that would follow. As they reached their targets, the skies behind them erupted in a crescendo of sound and a blaze of light, as German artillery launched Operation Barbarossa with a barrage along a front that stretched for 1,000 miles, from the Black Sea in the south to the shores of the Baltic in the north.

The momentum of the Germans' attack would carry them deep into the

8.000   2.770

24.000   3.300

BATTLE LINE-UP

12m   3m

20.000   7.100

heart of the Soviet Union. Hitler's plan was to strike at the capital, Moscow, in a short, sharp blitzkrieg – or lightning war. If Moscow fell, he believed, Russia would crumble. Time was of the essence: A lengthy campaign would trap the German army in the harsh Russian winter, when temperatures could drop so low that neither men nor machines could function properly. But although the campaign would be short, its aims were ambitious – the utter destruction of the mighty Soviet empire. In December 1940, Hitler spelled out just how overwhelming he wanted his victory to be: 'The bulk of the Russian army stationed in western Russia will be destroyed by daring operations led by deeply penetrating armored spearheads. Russian forces still capable of giving battle will be prevented from withdrawing into the depths of Russia.

'The enemy will be energetically pursued and a line will be reached from which the Russian airforce can no longer attack German territory. The final objective

Ewald von Kleist, leader of the German 1st Panzer Group (left). Soviet infantry march through Red Square, before Barbarossa (above right). Soviet propaganda urges Russians to destroy the invading fascists (below right).

COMMISSAR ORDER

In March 1941, Hitler shocked many senior officers when he declared: 'This struggle is one of ideologies and racial differences and will have to be conducted with unprecedented, unmerciful and unrelenting harshness…. The Commissars are the bearers of ideologies directly opposed to National Socialism. Therefore the Commissars will be liquidated. German soldiers guilty of breaking international law… will be excused. Russia has not participated in the Hague Convention and therefore has no rights to it.'

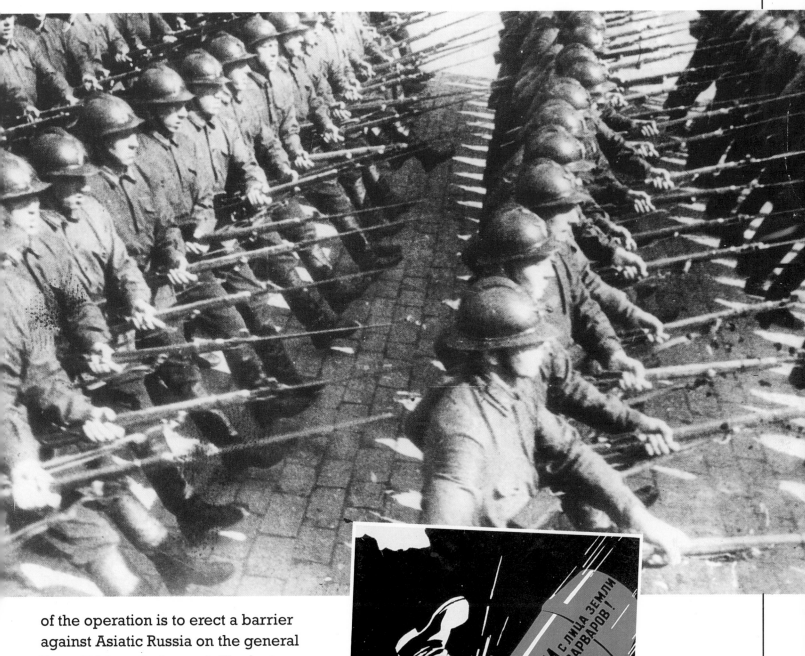

of the operation is to erect a barrier against Asiatic Russia on the general line of Volga–Archangel. The last surviving industrial areas of Russia in the Urals can then, if necessary, be eliminated by the Luftwaffe.'

It seemed an ideal time to go to war. The battle-hardened German troops had already fought successful campaigns in Norway, Denmark, Holland, Belgium, and France, and were led by supremely able officers. The Soviet Red Army, on the other hand, was in poor shape for war. The Russian leader Joseph Stalin – believing

that the military might eventually threaten to overthrow him – had deliberately weakened the army by executing or imprisoning many skilled high-ranking officers.

Despite Stalin's ruthless purge, however, the Red Army remained a fighting force to be reckoned with, if only for its vast size and massive reserves. Despite suffering heavy losses during the first six months of Barbarossa, at the end of 1941 it would still muster 400 divisions, comprising about 12 million men.

Russian aircraft and tanks, however, were no match for the more advanced weaponry their opponents enjoyed, and Hitler was also aware that his military command, control and communications systems, honed to a hard edge by recent experience, were far superior to those of the Red Army. The Russian troops had few radios, for instance, and relied heavily on field telephones and even semaphore flags.

Already confident of a positive outcome, Hitler's forces began to mass secretly in the east of Germany until, by the middle of June 1941, there were 118 frontline divisions assembled in three battle-groups. The northern group's objective in a three-pronged attack was to take the city of Leningrad, now St. Petersburg. Army Group South aimed for the Ukrainian city of Kiev, the port of Odessa on the Black Sea, the strategic Crimea peninsula, and ultimately, Stalingrad. The Russian capital of Moscow was the target of the central group. The clash of the titans was about to begin.

On June 22, the advance parties of Brandenburgers making for the vital bridges quickly captured their targets

BATTLE DIARY
BARBAROSSA

JUNE 1941
22 Beginning of Operation Barbarossa
29 Minsk pocket closed

JULY
1 Fall of Riga
5 German forces reach River Dnieper
9 Rivers Dvina and Dnieper crossed, Smolensk threatened
12 First Luftwaffe bombing raid on Moscow
14 German forces reach River Luga
17 Dnieper crossed at Mogilev
27 Smolensk pocket closed
31 Army Group North reaches Lake Ilmen

AUGUST
1 Russian counter-attack from the Pripet Marshes
7/8 First Russian air raid on Berlin
12 Army Group Centre splits to send Panzers north and south
23 Guderian heading rapidly towards Kleist
29 Finnish army captures Viipuri

SEPTEMBER
12 Kiev pocket closed
15 Leningrad cut off from the rest of the USSR
25 Start of the siege of Sevastopol
26 Kiev pocket eliminated – Germans now only 200 miles (320 km) from Moscow

Russian fighter aircraft lie wrecked on an airstrip (far left). Confident and keen, German infantrymen march through a Russian village in June 1941 (above), unaware of the levels of hardship they will face.
The contrasting face of defeat: A Soviet soldier, stunned by the speed and precision of the German advance, contemplates his gloomy future as a prisoner of war (left).

WarStories

Russian bravery was legendary. A dying Russian was seen crying while being tended. He explained that he was crying as he'd vowed to kill five fascists. The doctor said quickly, 'You killed at least 50 with your machine gun – I saw them falling!'

The city of Vitebsk as the Germans found it (below) – destroyed to delay them.

and defended them in readiness for the columns of panzer tanks that would arrive within the hour. As the sky lightened, they watched as an aerial armada of Heinkels, Dorniers and Stuka dive-bombers passed overhead, intending to neutralize the Russian air force on the ground.

The German tactic of blitzkrieg had been learned and practiced in their earlier invasions of Poland and western Europe. Speed was the key. And with crack regiments such as the Brandenburgers taking out strategic targets, and the relentless panzers rolling deep into enemy territory, it looked as though the Barbarossa campaign would be completed only a few weeks after it began.

In the far north, the advance of the Finnish army – Finland was an ally of Germany – took it up into the bleak, snowy wastes of the edge of the Arctic tundra.

Armed with Mauser rifles, German infantry move cautiously into a burning village on the first day of Operation Barbarossa, June 22, 1941 (above). Others hurry along a railroad track, during the fast and furious blitzkrieg (right).

Army Group North, meanwhile, under the command of Field Marshal Ritter von Leeb, swept northeast through the states of Latvia, Estonia and Lithuania. Historically often independent – and independent again today – these states bordering the Baltic Sea had been part of the Soviet Union since it was formed. Now the German invaders were met with mixed feelings. In Riga, the capital of Latvia, a teenager called Alex Baginskis witnessed the arrival of the Nazi troops:

'I was living in Riga with my mother. People were hoping that the Germans would come. They are our

historical enemies. They arrived with the Bible and the sword in the 12th and 13th centuries and subdued our people, forcing Christianity on them. They ruled us until World War I – but even the Germans would be better than the Russians.

'In June 1941, whispers started going around that the Soviets would deport people. These people were described by the Soviets as "socially dangerous". One night, over 35,000 people – out of a population of about 1,600,000 – were deported. Quite a number were shot as well. You can imagine the shock of going to visit my uncle next morning to find the whole house empty.

Blitzkrieg gathers momentum as German infantrymen prepare to storm a Soviet-occupied village in what had been eastern Poland, June 1941. They wait for an artillery bombardment to lift before advancing (above). A German infantry section shelters from Soviet fire and waits for a chance to advance, August 1941 (right).

STALIN'S ORGAN

The German's first felt the sting of 'Stalin's Organ' – a powerful artillery rocket launcher – in July 1941. They gave it a musical nickname because of the terrifying screech of its missiles. The Russians' name of 'Katyusha', taken from a popular song of the time, was a good deal more affectionate. One version had a range of up to 9,000 yards. The Germans were so frightened of the weapon that they promised to execute any Russian caught using it. Tactically, 'Katyusha' was very useful, but it did have one drawback. The dense cloud of smoke emitted when the rockets were launched was so noticeable that it almost always drew enemy artillery fire.

'A number of people, including my mother, took to the woods to stay with a family who lived near a farm. There were about 30 or 40 people there with us in the woods.

'About a week later the war began. Suddenly, early one morning, the German aircraft arrived over Riga. We were up on the roof, binoculars in hand, watching the dive-bombers and antiaircraft guns firing. The Germans didn't bomb the town – they bombed gas tanks, oil tanks.'

After the tyranny of Stalin's Soviet regime, the invaders were welcome. The Latvians went back to their homes to await the end of the fighting, even joining in to help throw the Soviets out.

'Within two days, the Red Army was retreating. We returned to Riga a couple of days after the Germans arrived. A home guard and scout troops were organized. I was a scout. There was still some hard fighting to do – there was a lot of street-fighting to do in Riga old town with the remaining Soviet troops or

Despite their determination and tough resistance, the war is over for these Soviet troops. Defeated and dejected, they are searched (above), and moved west to face captivity (left); these were familiar scenes of the summer of 1941.

TITANS CLASH

From June 1941, World War II entered a new phase of violence. For nearly two years, Hitler had kept his aggression to central and western Europe. Now the inevitable clash with communism had started, it was clear that this was to be a clash of titans. Hitler would not rest until he had wiped out communism; Stalin and the Russian people would fight to the bitter end. It was the beginning of total war.

TURNING POINT

Fear and apprehension in their faces, Soviet civilians find their shelter surrounded by the enemy (right); life will be harsh under Nazi rule.

East of Kiev, the Germans force their way on, devastation in their wake (below). Some 667,000 Soviet prisoners were captured in and around Kiev when the city's defenders surrendered.

local communist militia.'

But the Latvian people were too optimistic. It did not take long for the situation to turn for the worse. After the German troops came the German administration – the Nazi party. Hitler's officials had no intention of encouraging their enemy to enjoy their nationalism.

'At first everything was very patriotic - it was a feeling of relief. We all, even us kids, thought, "We're free now". The Latvian flag was everywhere. The honeymoon lasted for two or three months, before the German party people came and that was it.

'The national front was forbidden, national patriotic songs were forbidden, our anthem was forbidden. We were an occupied country again.'

The panzer spearhead of Army Group North surged

A Waffen SS division storm into action (right). Operation Barbarossa was the longest and most savage land battle ever fought.

A unit of German tanks, commandeered from the Czechoslovakians, thunder toward a bombed-out town, intent on continuing the destruction (right).

The Waffen SS Division 'Das Reich' arrive, marching through countryside in the heart of Russia (right). As yet, they are optimistic and not suffering the icy Russian winter, which will approach all too soon.

onward to the strategically important town of Dvinsk, around 220 miles from the German start point. There they were ordered to wait for other units to catch up – their advance did not resume until the beginning of July.

Meanwhile, the commander of Army Group Center, Field Marshal von Bock, headed for the Belorussian capital of Minsk, a stepping stone on the way to Moscow. Between him and the city lay the obstacle of the Bug River, but von Bock could not afford to be slowed down. Specially modified panzers – each equipped with a snorkel, tall air and exhaust vents – trundled up to 13 feet deep across the riverbed and established a bridgehead. Then sappers, or military engineers, could erect a pontoon bridge which allowed an armored column of more conventional vehicles to follow.

The attack took the Russians on the other side of the river completely by surprise. Confusion reigned among the defenders. German signalers intercepted a frantic Russian radio message: 'We are being fired on. What shall we do?' The disbelieving reply was, 'You must be insane.'

Moving at such a speed that the following infantry could not keep up –

Surrendering voluntarily, Russian soldiers grimly tear off their insignia and accept imprisonment (left). The Battle of Minsk is over and the city is in German hands. Stalin had General Pavlov executed as a result of this dramatic defeat.

Wearing heavy coats against the bitter winter, Red Army soldiers check over a Russian KV-1 (below), a strong, heavy but maneuverable tank which was first tested in 1940.

despite forced marches of up to 25 miles a day – two pincers of German armor swung north and south before encircling retreating Red Army forces, capturing some 300,000 troops. Meanwhile, the remainder of the group surrounded Minsk by June 27. The Germans then battled on to Smolensk, where they encountered fierce resistance before eventually razing the city.✍

The tactic of using panzers to puncture Red Army lines before surrounding and mopping up resistance was used repeatedly by the German military. Traveling at speed across the Russian countryside, the tank columns took on a strange beauty, as recorded by Curzio Malaparte, an Italian journalist who journeyed with Army Group South: 'The exhausts of the panzers belch out blue tongues of smoke. The air is filled with a pungent, bluish vapor that mingles with the damp green of the grass and with the golden reflection of the corn. Beneath the screaming arch of Stukas, the mobile columns of tanks resemble thin lines drawn with a pencil on the vast green slate of the Moldovian plain.'

Despite the overwhelming speed of the German advance, however, the huge distances it covered made it almost inevitable that some Russians slipped through the gaps and escaped capture. Dmitrii Gavyrushin, an infantry battalion commander, was among the many troops cut off behind the advancing German frontline, trapped by the blitzkrieg attack. His escape was to last an agonizing three months on the run.

'Having fought for 14 days without a break, I was bruised, but stayed in action. I was later wounded in the arm and hand. On July 24 I was put in the Mogilev hospital. On July 26, the town was captured by the fascists

A gaunt horse browses amongst the wreckage in the calm before the Germans come (above). Although the Russians fought with desperate ferocity, Marshal Budenny's defending army was forced to retreat, leaving behind a trail of abandoned Russian weapons and vehicles.

Small Russians towns such as this one grew accustomed to the arrival of German panzers (right). The more basic horse-drawn regiment 'Gross Deutschland' slowly proceeds along the muddy roads as a bitter Russian winter sets in (far right).

Red Army machine-gunners, heavily camouflaged in woodland greenery, lie in ambush (below). Despite Stalin's purge, the army was still a formidable force, full of brave, patriotic and determined soldiers.

and the hospital was not evacuated because it was encircled.'

Gavyrushin escaped from the hospital and went on the run disguised as a civilian, only to be captured once more before being sent to another hospital in Smolensk. Again he escaped and again he was recaptured, this time having reached the frontline near Shmakov. He and his fellow captives had to endure terrible conditions: 'After five hungry days, they put us in a truck and sent us forward. Hunger, and the pain of my wounds, stopped me keeping up with the fit ones, and I lagged behind, with the fascist escort all the time pushing me on with rifle-butt blows to my back. Having spent the night gathering our strength, we ran away in the morning. After several days, we reached the settlement of Stodolische and bumped into our surgeon. We asked him to change our bandages. He uncovered our wounds and they were already gangrenous, with little worms crawling out.'

Army Group South, meanwhile, led by Field Marshal Gerd von Rundstedt, advanced east

from southern Poland and Romania, meeting with ever fiercer resistance as it went. The largest tank battle of the war so far began on June 25 near Brody, when 1st Panzer Group clashed with no less than six Soviet mechanized corps. For four days, the two forces swayed back and forth across the steppes – the vast Russian plains – until superior German firepower, tactics and communication forced the Red Army to retreat east toward Kiev.

Hitler, however, was becoming increasingly frightened by the distances by which his

A Russian tank driver surrenders to his German captor, August 1941 (below). Men of the 'Der Führer' regiment, Waffen SS, wear improvised winter clothing (left).

Scenes of carnage in the streets of Rostov in southern Russia, as motorized and horse-drawn units of the German invasion force combine to take control (above).

At the edge of a Russian town under attack, German soldiers, barely under cover, prepare to open fire with a machine gun (above).

tanks were outstripping the infantry. The victorious panzers were ordered to halt. They delayed for three weeks, giving the defenders of the city of Leningrad precious time in which to prepare.

By the beginning of August, it appeared in Berlin that the Red Army, after suffering spectacular losses, was finished. But Hitler was receiving demands for reinforcements from some of his field commanders – difficult decisions between a number of competing priorities were called for. Both von Leeb in the north and von Rundstedt in the south needed extra resources, so Hitler ordered that the 3rd and 2nd Panzer Groups be diverted to help them. The reward would be enormous but the price was high, as both northern and southern groups became caught up in stubborn Russian resistance by Red Army units and also guerrilla fighters, or partisans.

A carefully prepared grave (below) shows that not all German soldiers enjoyed the rewards of a well fought crusade.

A group of German soldiers take some precious time off from their intensive, almost religious drive against the communist 'Untermenschen' (below). Unguarded, they are seen enjoying a taste of the local spirits.

БЬЕМСЯ МЫ ЗДОРОВО,
КОЛЕМ ОТЧАЯННО —
ВНУКИ СУВОРОВА,
ДЕТИ ЧАПАЕВА.

Eberhard Wagemann led a platoon of infantry in the advance into Russia. He recalls what a formidable adversary the Russian people could be:

'The partisan warfare, which was just then starting up, had been prepared and orchestrated, as it were, at arms' length by the Red Army and the Communist Party. I had taken over 9 Company from the wounded 1st Lieutenant Petersen by the Desna. Following the battle of Wjasma, I had been ordered to "clean out" an area of woodland with this company, after shots had been fired from there at our vehicles. As we got into the wood itself, we could see that the whole area was one large partisan camp, extended and occupied in peacetime. The paths had been covered over with camouflage netting – underground passageways linked bunkers and fighting positions, which were dug into and magnificently camouflaged in the overgrown forest floor. It was possible to mount an all-round defence of the area from the combat positions.

A Soviet propaganda poster uses inspiring images of Russian history, from Ivan the Terrible to the Revolution, to urge the citizens forward to victory (left). The appeal to nationalism rather than communism was effective, uniting the people against the common enemy and encouraging strong patriotic fervor.

Soviet workers put the finishing touches to part of an armored train – in the background is a T34 tank (above). Civilians grimly accompany a Soviet infantry unit as it marches out to face the enemy (left). Civilians were rarely informed of the fate of their menfolk.

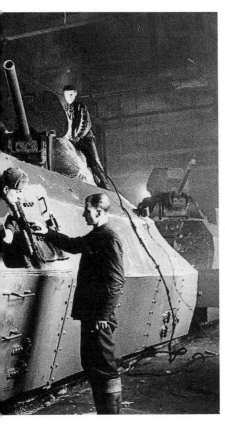

A young boy operates machinery in a munitions factory (above right). Everyone was required to do their bit as the German attack bit deep into Russia; the entire population was mobilized to help the war effort. Soviet citizens search for loved ones among the dead left after a German withdrawal (right).

ЕСЛИ ЗАВТРА ВОЙНА...

The legend on this 1938 Soviet propaganda poster is: 'If War Breaks Out tomorrow...' (left). The dead lie in the streets as cars and trams carry on in Leningrad (below left), during aerial bombardment, 1941. The city will see far greater suffering as the fighting rages on.

'At first sight the wood looked deserted – however, as the first volunteer stepped onto a ramp, he was shot in the stomach.

'The operation had to be called off – Stukas were called for.'

Despite such fierce and well-organized resistance, German troops and tanks crossed the Dnieper River in the south during mid-August and

The siege of Leningrad lasted over 900 days, causing great suffering to its inhabitants. As in Churchill's London, the people faced adversity with a practical response. Unable to get food from outside, city lawns where flowers had bloomed were given over to agriculture and soon became remarkable, not for floral displays, but cabbages.

In a German propaganda photograph, bewildered Russian children are gathered to give a public welcome to their German 'liberators', summer 1941 (left). A Soviet poster sneers that what mighty Napoleon failed to achieve in 1812, the rather pathetic leader, Hitler, would not achieve now (below).

began to battle northward in early September. Panzers from the north were making similar good progress south, until by mid-September a link had been forged.

The Soviet troops in and around the important city of Kiev, 130 miles to the west, fought fanatically but eventually succumbed on September 26, by which time they had virtually run out of ammunition. Thousands were killed and 667,000 prisoners were taken. The whole of the Ukraine now lay open to Hitler's troops but the weeks that had been lost would prove vital. When the advance on Moscow finally resumed, it came too late. The Russian winter was closing in.

THE BATTLE
FOR MOSCOW

The Germans would come within 20 miles of the capital of
Russia before they were halted by a last-ditch defense.

The winter of 1941 came earlier than anyone had expected – and was one of the most severe on record. The lubricating oil froze in vehicles' engines unless they were kept warmed; ungloved fingers were welded by the cold onto any bare metal surface; frostbite caused more casualties than enemy bullets; and sentries who slept at their posts risked death by exposure. And caught in the middle of conditions for which they were not prepared or equipped were the German armies, far from home, menacing the Russian capital of Moscow itself. Now they faced this new enemy – the ferocious cold of the Russian winter.

Red Army soldiers in winter camouflage loom out of the snow (far left). Both sides wore loose cotton smocks over everything else for snow camouflage. Their insignia, with hammer and sickle (left). Originally an antiaircraft gun, a German flak gun proves its worth in an antitank role on the Eastern Front (below). Later, such weapons were formidable weapon in desert campaigns as well (below).

It should never have been like this. By October 1941, Operation Barbarossa, Hitler's ambitious plan to smash the Soviet Union, had won great prizes for the German army as their blitzkrieg armor attacks led them into the heart of the Soviet empire: It seemed that victory was imminent. But the very speed of their advance and the great distances they had travelled caused serious problems for German commanders. Heavy demands had been made on Panzer tank forces, and the great encircling maneuvers by which they had attempted to trap the Red Army had rarely been entirely successful, often allowing large groups to escape to fight again.

Hitler's intention was to hold a strong frontline – preventing Russian forces from getting behind his troops – and attack the major Soviet cities of Leningrad and Moscow, the key prize. Leaving the siege of Leningrad in the north to his infantry, artillery and air force - the Luftwaffe – Hitler moved his tank forces from all over the Eastern Front to reinforce the panzer regiments near Moscow.

But months of bitter warfare with the retreating Red Army had left all the panzer regiments desperately understrength. Many vehicles were worn out by the

Equipped with loud speakers, a German car drives through devastated and burning ruins in Smolensk in October 1941, ordering the Russian troops to give up their weapons and surrender (above).

hundreds of miles they had driven. Disillusionment was also beginning to set in among their crews. One panzer commander spoke for many when he said: 'We still failed to find any real satisfaction in these achievements, for no-one was clear any longer what the actual aim of our strategy was or what higher purpose all these battles were supposed to serve.'

The delayed advance on Moscow – codenamed Operation *Taifun*, or Typhoon – began in earnest on October 2, 1941. The initial encounters went far better than many officers had feared. The first blow, spearheaded by 2nd Panzer Group, fell on the city of Bryansk, southwest of Moscow, and the tanks soon raced on to link up with General Maximilian von Wiech's Second Army.

But the Germans found themselves facing a more formidable foe than before. The delay before the attack had enabled the Soviets to marshal their

War **S**tories

Much has been written about the Soviet Russians' grim outlook and lack of humor, but Marshal Budenny belied this stereotype. Once, he was reported to have thrown caution – along with his medals and uniform – to the wind, and bathed naked in a vat of wine with a group of similarly unclad women.

The leader of the 4th Armored Group, General Erich Hopner, discusses the German advance with one of his men, Russia, October 1941 (right).
'Everything for the Front, Everything for Victory!' A group of Russian partisans gathers to receive weapons (above).

forces. To save Moscow, Stalin had called on Marshal Georgi Zhukov, a tough and wily general who had already helped defend Leningrad. But the old general's summary of the situation was bleak: 'There was no longer a continuous front in the west, and the large gaps could not be closed because the command had run

German infantrymen advance through smoke on the trail for Moscow, a blaze of destruction from one of the Luftwaffe's aerial attacks glowing behind them (above): Later the icy winter slows down the Nazi advance (right). A Nazi soldier carrying a Mauser rifle throws a stick grenade during an assault (below).

out of reserves.' Finding a trusted general who had recently retreated from Kiev, Zhukov asked what defenses guarded the road to Moscow. 'When I came through there,' the general replied, 'I saw only three policemen.'

Zhukov set about reorganizing what was left of the Red Army reserve forces and recruiting civilians, using them to fill gaps wherever possible. Among these new soldiers were those commanded by M. A. Zashibalov, who recalls how his division helped defend Moscow after

Soviet antiaircraft gun crewmen anxiously cover the advance of their troops against Luftwaffe attack (below). They are well camouflaged and well insulated, in contrast to the badly prepared German troops now suffering the vicious winter.

German horse-drawn transport makes slow, painful progress through appalling winter conditions (above). Hitler had expected to be victorious long before the winter.

only a brief training in the 'Peoples' Reinforcement' – a rapidly recruited civilian army.

'The enemy began an offensive against Tarusa and Serpukhov. The 49th Army HQ did not have enough reserves to defend these towns and an operational "gateway" 18 to 25 miles wide began to form, undefended either by troops or defense obstacles.

'Luckily for us, the German–fascist command was so drunk with success that it did not always carry out a proper tactical or operational reconnaissance, and therefore it had no idea of the favorable situation which was developing in this sector.'

Zashibalov's division force marched into position to

fill the alarming gap that had developed: 'With such a length to be defended, our density on the ground was not, of course, very great. We had one soldier for every 100 to 160 yards of front, and one heavy machine gun for every two miles.'

The Soviet position remained grim. German forces continued to encircle and capture Russians in their hundreds of thousands. The end seemed near: One invader observed, 'Prisoners told us that this new attack, launched so late in the year, had been completely unexpected. Moscow seemed about to fall into our hands.'

The commander of Army Group North, Field Marshal von Leeb (second from right), plots the campaign with General Hopner (second from left), Commander of the 4th Panzer Army, Russia 1941 (above). The comparative strengths of the invading German army and the Red Army defenders in October 1941 (right).

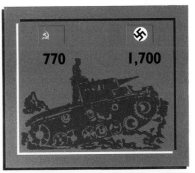

950   1,400

770   1,700

BATTLE LINE-UP

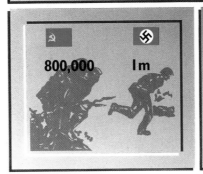

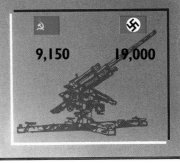

800,000   1m

9,150   19,000

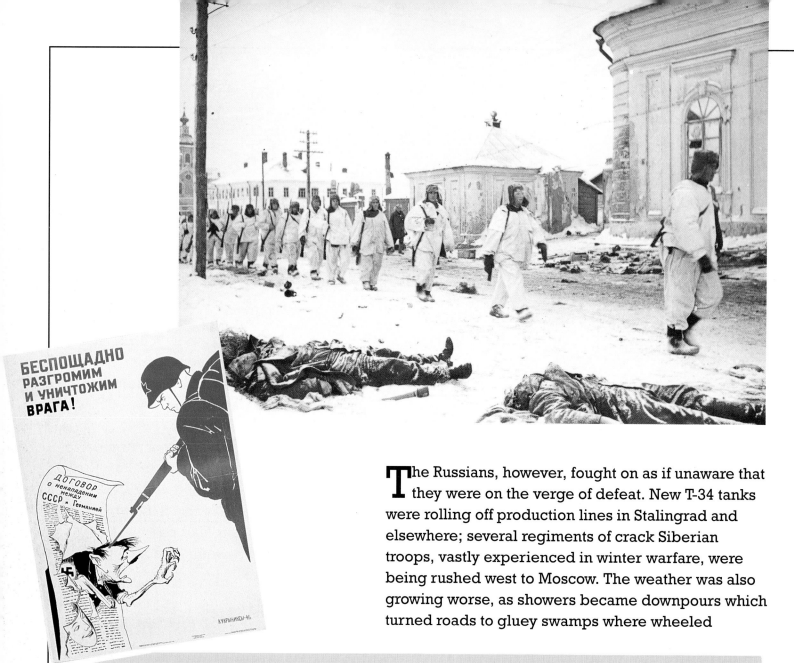

The Russians, however, fought on as if unaware that they were on the verge of defeat. New T-34 tanks were rolling off production lines in Stalingrad and elsewhere; several regiments of crack Siberian troops, vastly experienced in winter warfare, were being rushed west to Moscow. The weather was also growing worse, as showers became downpours which turned roads to gluey swamps where wheeled

MARSHAL GEORGI ZHUKOV

The greatest Soviet military leader of World War II was born in 1896. He enlisted with the fledgling Red Army in October 1918 and joined the Bolshevik Party a year later. During the 1930s he became a forthright supporter of armored warfare, and in 1939 conducted a successful campaign against the Japanese in Manchuria. In World War II he was entrusted with the defence of Leningrad after the German invasion, before being moved to the Moscow front. In 1942 he was in overall command of the Soviet forces defending Stalingrad and later played a major role in the Battle of Kursk in 1943, and the drive on Berlin in 1945.

Kalinin, northwest of Moscow, December 1941. Russian troops in winter uniform march past the bodies of their German enemies with a hardened indifference (above left). A Russian poster (far left): No mercy will be shown to the evil dictator who has committed such atrocities.

In bleak scenery, German troops mount assaults on Russian villages, crouching in the snow under the cover of their panzer tanks (above and right).

*The brilliant panzer
commander, General Erich
von Manstein, pictured in the
Crimea, 1942 (above).
Christmas far from home – a
rare and happy rest from
hostilities (inset). A German
message to the Russian people
(below left); they should
welcome Nazi 'liberation'. A
brief glimmer of warmth in
the push toward Moscow
(above right). German
soldiers enjoy rare warmth,
while others share a cigarette
(far right)*

War Stories

A successful supply drop was cause for celebration among the German forces. Imagine then, the anticlimax amongst the men, when on one occasion the eagerly awaited bundles were ripped open, only to reveal one of the few things for which they had absolutely no use – two tons of condoms.

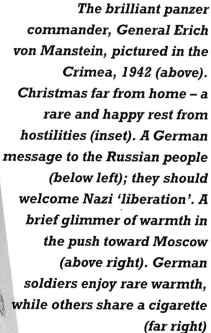

vehicles got bogged down. Around the corner lay the Soviets' greatest ally: The bitter cold of deep winter.

While the Russian spirits rose, many of the German troops were showing signs of exhaustion. Nearly all had been fighting continuously since June, and some had taken part in the Balkan campaign before that. Their equipment was failing and Guderian, the tank commander, reported that, of the 600 tanks with which his panzer group had commenced the invasion, only 50 remained serviceable. Russian partisans – or guerrilla freedom fighters – were taking a heavy toll on German supply convoys. The early promise of October was rapidly fading, leaving the Germans with little choice other than to dig in for the winter.

Winter came abruptly, halting the advance of 3rd and 4th panzer groups in the north. One of their generals noted: 'About November 20, the weather suddenly broke and almost overnight the full fury of

WINTER CLOTHING

At the beginning of the Russian campaign, the only winter clothing available to the German forces were standard double-breasted, calf-length gray greatcoats, together with leather marching boots and woollen gloves. During the winter of 1941, a wide variety of Russian civilian clothing was used, including quilted jackets, fur waistcoats and fur hats. Later a proper gray and white two-piece reversible blanket-lined suit was issued, together with a fur-lined cap with ear flaps. Soviet troops also wore double-breasted greatcoats, called kaftans. With them they wore quilted collarless jackets and trousers, thick felt boots, wadded with straw, and the *schlem*, a peaked, pointed cloth helmet with ear flaps.

the Russian winter was upon us.'

Nevertheless, the two panzer groups edged toward Moscow with increasing difficulty, and on December 2 a supporting infantry division found a gap in the defenses. By driving through the night, it managed to enter the western outskirts of the Russian capital. The heart of the city – and of the Soviet Union – lay only 20 miles ahead.

But the advance was almost the last straw for the attackers, as *Unterscharführer* Streng, a member of the crack SS, remembers: 'We could only advance step by step toward our final destination – Moscow.... Many of the soldiers had managed to steal Russian overcoats and fur hats and were hardly recognizable as Germans anymore. All our winter clothing had been infested with lice and was impossible to wear. To keep the engines running, we had to light fires underneath the sumps. Some of the fuel had frozen, the engine oil had thickened and we had no glysanthine to stop drinking water freezing.'

Within the capital, Muscovites had adopted increasingly desperate tactics to defend their

REPRIEVE

On August 4, 1941, Hitler told his generals to divert their panzers from Moscow and head north and south toward Leningrad and Kiev respectively. General Guderian pointed out that Moscow now lay open to attack, but the Führer was adamant. These diversions gave defenders of Moscow the respite they needed to hold the capital.

TURNING POINT

A poster praises the partisans – the Geman advance meets continued opposition (left). Undeterred by the heavy blast of German shells, a Russian medic helps a wounded soldier (right). Ceremony amid chaos: Russian troops on parade in Red Square, November 1941, mark the anniversary of the 1917 revolution (below) – then march on to the front nearby.

city: 'Moscow had opened the prisons and had armed the released prisoners. In the factories, workers' brigades had been assembled. Women and children were put in to dig trenches.'

The German troops could not support their positions, and the following day they were repulsed by tanks. Streng and his companions marked the closest the Germans would come to their goal: The drive for Moscow had failed.

The Red Army attack (above). Armed with a submachine gun, a Red Army soldier urges his comrades on (below). German soldiers enjoy the snow (above right). A German infantryman (below right).

In bitter winter conditions, Zhukov struck back, launching offensives from north and south of Moscow on December 6, spearheaded by newly

assembled 'shock armies'.

German supply lines were overstretched and the Luftwaffe's attempts to airlift supplies often missed their targets – many airdrops fell into grateful Russian hands. In Germany, Propaganda Minister Joseph Goebbels began a 'clothes for the troops' drive, in order to afford soldiers some protection against the extreme temperatures. But although the campaign resulted in the donation of thousands of fur coats, the terrible winter was almost at an end by the time they began arriving in the east.

In contrast, the Red Army was generally much better off, being more suitably dressed and better acclimatized to the harsh cold. But Zhukov was still not getting all the tanks he needed, and those which did arrive often had to be crewed by men with only a few hours' training.

Despite the odds facing his troops, Hitler ordered that there could be no withdrawal. Some of his commanders thought the order insane, but in any case the terrible weather conditions prevented retreats of more than a few miles a night. Instead the Germans dug in, surrounded by artillery bristling out toward the enemy on all sides.

An SS doctor remembers the view from his unit's

protected position: 'Suddenly I heard the unmistakable noise of the Russian rocket shells, the so-called Stalin's Organs. They were definitely meant for us, for everybody disappeared suddenly into cover holes. Since I hadn't dug one myself, I couldn't disappear without a trace. So I quickly threw myself behind a tree and watched the beautiful display of rocket shells crashing down. I will never forget the sinister black, red and violet flare from the shells.'

Zhukov despatched ski troops behind German lines to harry the enemy, together with cossacks and paratroops. Partisan activity was already causing the stranded invaders problems. But some of the Russian frontline tactics were suicidal. Wave upon wave of infantry would run from the cover of the mists toward German positions, only to be cut down by machine guns and mortars, until Zhukov had to issue an order

With all motorized vehicles frozen up, German troops are reduced to using horse-drawn wagons, stolen from the Russians, for their advance (left). The 'Grossdeutschland' Division waits with anticipation as mail from home is distributed, a small but welcome comfort (below, left).

Although badly injured, a communist commissar orders his troops forward against the Germans (above). The German army in retreat: Soldiers who had been fighting in summer uniforms are forced to improvise camouflage with stolen tablecloths and bed linen, in an attempt to avoid Soviet snipers (left).

Only a few German units had skis – and all had to make their own snow camouflage clothing (above right). Blending in to the background, Soviet soldiers lay a mine on a railroad line (above left).

forbidding such head-on charges.

Despite great losses, the Red Army gradually dislodged the enemy. The 2nd Panzer Group had little option but to pull back, abandoning valuable resources: Tractors, weapons, and even tanks. A fortnight later, an angry Hitler sacked the group's commander.

Kluge's Fourth Army was also under sustained

pressure. Kluge, too, had decided to withdraw, but a direct order from Hitler stopped him. By Christmas Eve, 1941, his position was extremely precarious: His headquarters was defended from the Red Army only by the 50 surviving tanks of the 19th Panzer Division. Other formations were in even worse shape: One commander's four panzer divisions retained fewer than 15 tanks apiece.

An unexpected respite came for the German Army Group Center when Russian attacks against it faltered to a standstill, the troops too tired to advance any further. But Zhukov was not completely done. On the night of January 7, 1942, he launched an offensive from north of Moscow in an attempt to cut off the German troops besieging Leningrad.

In the middle of a blizzard, four Russian armies threw their combined weight against the German 16th Army, inflicting such heavy casualties that the German line was held almost solely by SS General Theodor Eicke's 3rd *Totenkopf,* or Death's-head, Division. Over the next three months, their resistance was an epic of courage and determination.

The division had already suffered heavily in the

Red Army men surge forward, determined to win back a small Russian town (above).
Known to the Red Army as the 'flying tank' – and to the Germans as the 'Black Death' – a Russian antiaircraft gun defends the skies above Moscow (below).

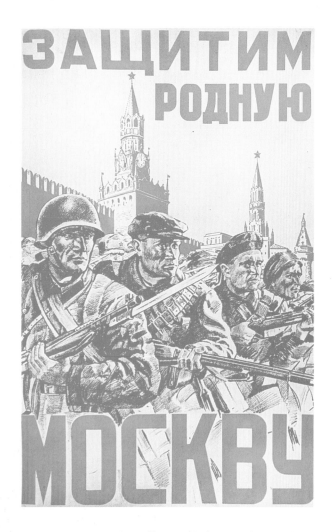

A patriotic poster depicts the three Russian armed forces and makes a determined pledge to defend Moscow to the last man (above).

summer and fall fighting, losing nearly 9,000 casualties – roughly 50 percent of its strength – only half of which had been replaced. But they had two advantages. The SS had been more far-sighted than the army, ensuring that large stocks of warm winter parkas, boots and hats had been issued to its men. Moreover, they had constructed bunkers and trenches in the Valdai Hills, a natural defensive position.

Nevertheless, by January 20 the *Totenkopf* was almost completely cut off. Eicke had to order all his walking wounded back from field hospital into the frontline. German companies fought off attacks from

vastly larger Russian forces: The only villages the Russians recaptured were those in which every *Totenkopf* soldier lay dead.

By the end of February only isolated groups of German troops fought on, separated by the wilderness and the enemy from their comrades. They could no longer evacuate their wounded and the Luftwaffe had become their only means of supply. Yet still the invasion force managed to hold out.

Then, in the second week of March, the weather began improving and the supply situation eased. Attempts were made to relieve survivors and large airborne attacks again became possible. Flight

Despair and resignation on the faces of Russian civilians (above). The suffering of the Russian people, young and old, knew no bounds. Crushed by the German invaders, harsh winter and severe shortage of supplies, the future seems to hold only the promise of endless misery. Their resilience was remarkable.

LENINGRAD UNDER SEIGE

'A dog or a cat was worth a month's salary on the black market. Money no longer had any real value.' Food was the only thing that counted. In November 1941, Leningrad was virtually encircled by von Leeb's Army Group North and had endured almost constant artillery bombardment since the fall. When this siege was lifted, after 900 days, only one third of the original 3,000,000 people had survived.

The first winter accounted for some ten percent of this total casualty list. The Germans and Finns closed off all access, except for a narrow lifeline over the frozen Lake Ladoga to the nearest railroad 352 km away. Convoys of trucks crossing were bombed continuously, but supplies still got through. When the thaw came, people grew vegetables on every clear patch of ground and boats replaced the trucks across the lake. The first railroad train was greeted in the city with a cheer in February 1943.

A gaunt man grimly clutches his meager bread ration (left). During the siege of Leningrad, rations were cut to 12 ounces of bread a day for workers and half that for those not in a regular job. Electricity was severely rationed and only essential telephone services maintained.

An elderly pensioner takes over the job in a factory that his son had done before he joined the army (inset left). The unparalleled suffering endured by the Soviet people over almost three years remains a testament to their fortitude.

Sergeant Alfred Sticht, an observer in a Heinkel 111, tells of one dangerous bombing raid his plane made on Moscow: 'Another machine is caught in the brilliant glare of the searchlight. In a flash, several other searchlights pounce on the aircraft. I can see through the telescope it's a Heinkel 111 – it's one of ours. He's making frantic attempts to escape the clutches of the searchlight – in vain.

'A searchlight grazes us, then loses us, but it's soon back again. The glare of more than thirty searchlights fix on us. The flak fires from every barrel. Shells go off all around us.

'There's a huge bang, then a flash of fire. Our machine is shaking – we've been hit. I prime the bombs and then pull the emergency cord. There's a giant column of fire below us... The engines are

Russian soldiers carry out an exercise in a Moscow boulevard (above). At noon on Sunday June 22, 1941, citizens of Moscow hear Foreign Commissar Molotov announce over a loudspeaker that the Germans have invaded (right). Above the streets of Moscow, an air defense squad watches for Luftwaffe aircraft (below).

Joseph Stalin, an aloof, apparently infallible, dictator commands Soviets to continue to face up to the hardships and stand firm to repel the invaders (above). Stalin was regarded as an all-powerful, almost godlike, leader by his people.

screaming. "Is anyone wounded?" Everybody reports they're OK.'

It was not until April 14, with spring in the air, that the weary *Totenkopf* troops were able to make their way back through the Russian lines. On April 22, 1942, after 73 days in isolation, they joined up with German forces by crossing the icy waters of the Lovat River, swollen by the thawing snow.

The German army had failed to take Moscow, but Zhukov had not succeeded in throwing it right back. After a pause for regrouping and re-equipping, the German offensive would begin again. Moscow had been saved – by only 20 miles. When the Germans advanced again, Moscow was no longer the target. Their goal would lie further to the south: Stalingrad, the gateway to the Caucasus.

Women in the Urals work producing cartridges (left). Just as in Britain, the war effort demanded the involvement of everyone.

War Stories

Astonished by his staunchly anticommunist employer's willingness to help Russia, Churchill's private secretary asked him how he could give his support. The answer was unequivocal: 'I have only one purpose – the destruction of Hitler, and my life is much simplified thereby.'

A spectacular display of antiaircraft fire lights up the night sky over Moscow as the Luftwaffe attack (below left).

A cartoon in the window of the Soviet news agency, Tass's, in July 1941, predicts what the fascist invasion will mean (right). Soviets are urged to cut power lines, blow up bridges, destroy supplies and fire on Nazi troops, to thwart the enemy advance (far left).

STALINGRAD

Although the German army overran Stalingrad, the city's defenders took refuge among the ruins and fought back amid the rubble of their homes. The invaders found themselves besieged in the city they had conquered.

The Germans fighting in the ruins of the Russian city of Stalingrad had a word for the type of battle they found themselves in: *Rattenkrieg,* the 'war of the rats'. Among the bombed-out streets, the enemy was everywhere: In cellars, in derelict houses, beneath wrecked vehicles. The struggle was at close quarters, between groups of men who used guns, bayonets, and fingernails, clawing through timber and rubble to reach each other. Advances were measured in feet and inches. The enemy could be lurking on the other side of the street – or the other side of a wall.

Shrouded in smoke, the suburbs of Stalingrad lie before German attackers (below). Grain elevators, visible against the skyline, will be hotly contested killing grounds. Machine-gun support for troops moving in (left). The arm badge worn by a Russian Marshal (right).

BATTLE LINE-UP

1,000,500   1,011,500

13,541   10,290

MANEATER

France
Greece
Jugoslavia
Rumania
Poland
Belgium

After the German army's failure to take Moscow in 1941, and its desperate struggle to hold a defensive line through the winter, Hitler changed his objectives. The attack on Moscow would not be resumed; instead, the German spring and summer offensive in 1942 would fall in the south. The aim was to capture the Crimea Peninsula on the Black Sea, and then to launch a two-pronged drive toward the city of Stalingrad, today called Volgograd, to the east and the Caucasus Mountains to the south. Stalingrad's factories were churning out roughly a quarter of all

War Stories

When the Germans sent out patrols against partisans, they deliberately put nonsmokers at the front. This was due to their acute sense of smell, which helped them pinpoint the whereabouts of partisans by the pungent odor of Russian tobacco, which lingered in the air after the partisans had passed.

Russia's tanks and other armored vehicles; and the Caucasus oilfields supplied vital oil and gas. If Hitler had failed to defeat the Red Army head on, he could cut off its lifeblood.

The drive to Stalingrad – codenamed *Fall Blau,* or Case Blue – began on June 28, 1942, with Army Group South divided in two for the push. Group B, on the northern flank, would strike toward the mighty Volga River that flowed through the city, after first clearing the banks of the Don River. Meanwhile, Group A would head southeast to seize the Caucasus oilfields. The plan – though it offered great prizes – was fraught with danger from the beginning. German army chiefs saw right away that Army Group B's drive east would leave a long left flank exposed to attack from the north – and it was protected only by Hungarian, Romanian, and Italian troops of low morale and dubious ability. In its sheer ambition, *Fall Blau* already held the seeds of the biggest defeat Hitler's Third Reich had yet sustained.

To begin with it looked as though the lightning attack – or blitzkrieg – was working as planned, as German Panzers and Stukas caught the Russians off balance. But the initial attack was blunted by fanatical Russian resistance around the town of Voronezh on the Don River, and German forces finally reached Stalingrad late in August 1942. The city had been greatly reinforced, but throughout the day and night of August 23, it suffered the single largest bombardment ever launched by the Luftwaffe – the German air force – against one target. By dawn next day, the city was a raging inferno. The glow of the flames could be seen by panzer troops stationed 30

German engineers construct a bridge over a stream bed (far left) to aid the German advance, which continues by panzer tank (top far left) and by motorcycle (bottom far left). Yet the majority of German transport and artillery was horse drawn during the Russian campaign (below). General Hoth watches his division set off for the Don River, June 1942 (inset). A propaganda poster (inset far left).

German Sixth Army tanks wait to cross the Don River (right). Most of the tankmen will not return.

THE EIGHT-MONTH SIEGE

Before the German army could resume its eastward drive in 1942, it had to secure the fortified Black Sea port of Sevastopol, from where Russian troops could strike at the German flank. It was first attacked in November 1941 but did not fall until June next year, after 247 days. The grim determination of the defenders was indicative of what was to come at Stalingrad, but the warning was lost in euphoria at the Russian surrender.

miles away. One German soldier wrote to his wife, 'All of us feel that the end, victory, is near.'

For the attackers, Stalingrad held two particular targets: The city's industrial northern sector and the power plant in the south. While many women and children were evacuated from the devastated city under cover of darkness, its remaining civilians were mobilized to try and hold the Germans back around a defensive line within the city itself. In Stalin's words, they would make the city an 'impregnable fortress'.

Within the wrecked city, any shelter offered safety. One young girl hid in a cellar for 163 days with three other children and three women, creeping out to

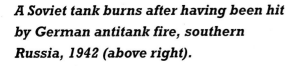

A Soviet tank burns after having been hit by German antitank fire, southern Russia, 1942 (above right).

The Germans approach the crucial target of Stalingrad in the summer of 1942 (right). The planned drive on the city, Fall Blau, was fraught with danger from the outset, and was to result in a damaging defeat.

German soldiers deploy a light infantry support gun during street fighting (left). A machine-gun team moves forward to take up a firing position (above right). German infantry advance, the burning city in the background (below right). Stalingrad suffered the largest bombardment ever launched by the Luftwaffe on August 23, 1942.

War Stories

After nine attempts to blow up a bridge over which German tanks would pass, a Russian partisan took across her baby, wrapped up with a time bomb. Halfway over, she stopped to change her tot's diaper and fixed the bomb to a girder. Three hours later the bridge blew up.

BATTLE DIARY
STALINGRAD

JANUARY 1942
18- Timoshenko's winter offensive
31
JUNE
28 Opening of Army Group South's summer offensive
AUGUST
11 Sixth Army reaches the Don
23 XIV Panzer Corps reaches Stalingrad
SEPTEMBER
2 Beginning of battle for Stalingrad
NOVEMBER
19 Beginning of Soviet

counteroffensive
23 Sixth Army surrounded in Stalingrad
DECEMBER
12- Manstein's relief attempt fails
24
JANUARY 1943
10 Beginning of final Soviet offensive to take Stalingrad
31 Paulus surrenders
FEBRUARY
2 Last German forces in Stalingrad surrender

forage for food: 'I had to walk, run, and crawl about 200 yards over open ground. The snow was coated with ash because the factory zone had burned for several days. It was terrifying, crawling past the body of Nastya, the old woman who was our neighbor, lying not far from the scorched tree where the children of our street used to play.

'I trod past a field kitchen. There was an unusually tasty smell in the air. Pea soup, probably, made from concentrates. I couldn't make up my mind to knock on the door of the dugout. We knew that the soldiers' rations had been cut from day to day.

'"Where do you come from, little girl?" In front of me stood a soldier in a white sheepskin coat and fur

General Chuikov (above, second from left), commander of the Soviet 62nd Army, in his command post at Stalingrad. General Chuikov was responsible for defending the city throughout the hard-fought battle. German troops enter the rubble remains of the Barrikady factory, scene of bitter fighting during October 1942 (below).

cap.... The captain took my small empty bucket. I suddenly grew happy. The officer slid some food cubes into my bucket. At first I wanted to cry, but in our cellar there had been a kind of unwritten law against crying.'

In the streets, the German army's tactical superiority was useless to soldiers engaged in one-on-one

Soviet gunners fire into quickly deteriorating German positions during the Red Army counterattack in the Caucasus, summer 1942, to stop the seizure of the oilfields (above). The consistently heavy German bombing during the battle for Stalingrad reduced the prosperous city on the Volga to a pile of rubble (right). The winter proves a valuable ally to the Soviets, who begin to root the Germans out, January 1943 (left).

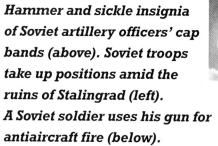

Hammer and sickle insignia of Soviet artillery officers' cap bands (above). Soviet troops take up positions amid the ruins of Stalingrad (left). A Soviet soldier uses his gun for antiaircraft fire (below).

combat. And the attackers were without their top elite forces, most of whom had been withdrawn to France for rest. On September 2, the Sixth Army advanced to relieve the isolated XIV Panzer Corps, while the Soviet armies withdrew to positions within the city. The 'war of the rats' began in earnest.

The Germans could have no real hope of winning such a war of attrition. The panzer commanders were anxious that their tank strength was being frittered away in house-to-house fighting as they tried to clear the city – a task that would have been far better left to the infantry. The tanks would be needed if the Soviets launched a counterattack.

Still Hitler insisted that there was to be no retreat. Things appeared to be going well: By September 26, the swastika flew from the top of the government buildings in the central Red Square. But victory was

Soviet infantry advance in search of signs of German resistance which, by this time, is almost extinguished (above). Soviet snipers take cover in Stalingrad ruins (right).

TURNING POINT

POOR STRATEGY

The German summer offensives of 1942 showed the weakness of Hitler as a strategist. His decision to attack the Caucasus oilfields, aiming eventually for a linkup with General Rommel's army in the Middle East, was overambitious and ran the risk of Soviet counterstrikes. Ultimately, such bold aims were beyond the powers of the German forces.

A Red Army soldier inspects ammunition left by retreating Germans (right). Despite heavy losses on the frontline, Red Army antitank riflemen put on a good display, August 1942 (below right).

an illusion. The city's defenders were being kept supplied by a constant stream of ferries from the eastern side of the Volga River, while Marshal Georgi Zhukov – the saviour of Moscow, now in charge also of Stalingrad – kept his armies up to strength by sending in fresh troops to replace casualties. The German Sixth Army lost 40,000 men by October 6: Although the Soviet casualties were probably much higher – official figures have never been released – his massive reserves gave Zhukov the edge.

During the second week in October, the German commander General Friedrich Paulus received a few reinforcements. His targets were unlikely ones: Two tractor factories and the city's grain elevators. At the latter, Andrei Khozyanyov, a Soviet officer, saw fierce fighting: 'At noon, 12 enemy tanks came up from the south and west. We had already run out of ammunition for our antitank rifles, and we had no grenades left. The tanks approached the

BOMBER GIRL

'Ever since I was a small child, I had always dreamt of becoming a pilot....' Nadia Fedutenko, a major in the Red Army's air force, began as a civilian pilot flying dangerous missions for Military Intelligence. Transferred to the air force, she was commissioned as a squadron leader in the Raskovoy regiment, which flew dive-bombers. The regiment saw heavy action over Stalingrad, during which Nadia was wounded whilst on a mission to destroy enemy artilley positions. Only a few seconds from the target, her copilot noticed blood streaming from under her helmet, but Nadia asserted: 'It is nothing, I will withstand it. You just make sure you aim more precisely.' The task was completed successfully and only when she had reported this did she allow herself to be taken to hospital.

Nadia Fedutenko, Russian dive-bomber ace, who made her name in a role of danger (above); with some of her ground crew (right). In the cockpit of her plane, Nadia embarks on another mission (below).

German infantrymen prepare for battle at the Barrikady factory (right). Tension and the strain of perpetual vigilance show in their faces as they continue their hopeless mission to take and hold Stalingrad. Around them, the city is reduced to desolation (far right).

Wiking

Moving through the ruins of a building in Stalingrad, a group of German infantrymen pause on hearing an explosion too close for comfort (right).

elevator from two sides and began to fire at our garrison at point-blank range. But no-one flinched. Our machine guns and tommy guns continued to fire at the enemy's infantry, preventing them from entering the elevator. Then a Maxim machine gun, together with a gunner, was blown up by a shell, and the casing of the second Maxim was hit by shrapnel, bending the barrel. We were left with one light machine gun. Fighting flared up inside the building. We sensed and heard the enemy soldiers' breath and footsteps, but we could not see them in the smoke.'

By the end of October, the Sixth Army effectively controlled the city, with only isolated Russian pockets of resistance. But General Paulus was stretched to his limit and his final effort to clear the city on November 10 failed, with horrific casualties.

At 7:20 A.M. on the freezing cold morning of November 19, a 3,500-gun barrage heralded the Soviet counteroffensive, aimed at the hapless Romanian Third Army northwest of Stalingrad.

Flying overhead that morning was Hans Rudel, the Luftwaffe's most highly decorated pilot: 'What troops are those coming toward us?' he wondered. 'Masses in brown uniform – are they Russians? No. They are Romanians. Some of them are even throwing away their rifles in order to be able to run faster.'

More than 500 Russian tanks swept the enemy aside. By November 21, Soviet troops were menacing Paulus from the rear; meanwhile, other Soviet forces had sealed Stalingrad, so that though it controlled the city, the Sixth Army was also trapped within it.

Sergeant Ivan Morotskii commanded a mortar unit besieging the German forces during the last weeks before they were driven out of Stalingrad: 'I remember meeting some local women. "We don't need anything," they said, "except something to eat. The Germans have eaten the last cat and dog."

'One dawn we saw German aircraft flying low, and they mistook us for their own beleaguered troops. They dropped provisions by parachute and this manna from heaven was just what we wanted.

'In one settlement we captured a

The emblem and armband of the 5th SS Panzer Division (left), and one of its heroes, Siegfried Melinkat, an 18-year-old corporal, wearing the Iron Cross (below).

German POWs trudge into captivity, their resistance having crumbled (below). At the end of the siege, there were more than 100,000 dead and 90,000 taken prisoner.

motorized battalion and the headquarters of some German formation. There were vehicles loaded with safes containing Iron Crosses.

'Along the road, broken and holed, here and there stood wrecked enemy equipment, and piles of abandoned belongings. The one-time immaculate all-conquering Hitlerite army was in retreat. On the way we often met columns of prisoners, escorted by our men.

'It was quite a sight how they looked. Some wore women's dresses and blouses and substitute over-boots made of straw. They were dirty, with frozen faces, and without the slightest spark of life shining in their eyes.'

Serious German resistance crumbled. On January 31, 1943 – the morning after Paulus learned that he had been promoted to field marshal – Russian troops were outside his command bunker. With little choice, he ordered the radio and coding equipment to be destroyed and then surrendered.

Some 90,000 officers and men of the once-proud Sixth Army began the long march east to Siberia and captivity. Their suffering was far from over: Only 7,000 would survive their ordeal to return home – but not for another ten years.

The disaster of Stalingrad profoundly shocked the German people and armed forces alike. Never before had such a large force perished so terribly. Although they had suffered defeats before, they were on a smaller scale and the Germans had always resumed the offensive. With Stalingrad this tide was turned, and although the war was by no means over, the period of German victories was coming to a close.

A Red Army man and some Russian women emerge from underground bunkers amid the utter desolation of a residential suburb outside Stalingrad. Many locals sheltered underground throughout the brutal winter battle, surviving on what little food they could scrounge (above).

KURSK

A last stand by Hitler's troops would try to entrap the
advancing Red Army on the Russian plains – the steppes –
which would see one of history's largest tank battles.

The consequences of disobeying an order from Adolf Hitler could be serious. The ruthless Führer, or leader, was the most powerful man in Germany, and the supreme commander of all the German armed forces. And, after failing to take Moscow in 1941 and being forced to withdraw from Stalingrad in 1942, Hitler was growing impatient with his army commanders in the East. Yet in February 1943, SS General Paul Hausser, encircled by the Red Army in the Russian town of Kharkov, took the decision to ignore a senseless order from the Führer. Georg Berger, a communications officer in Hausser's corps, had a close view of his commander's uncomfortable position:

'The order from the Führer on February 13 was curt and simple, "Kharkov is to be held". Hausser requested permission to evacuate the town, which was rejected. However, Field Marshal von Manstein empowered Hausser to seek direct contact with the Führer's HQ in order to give his own explanation of how precarious the situation was.

In the late afternoon of February 14, Paul Hausser came out of the cramped farmhouse into the cold and paced up and down in silence. Turning, he said calmly, "Give out the orders to the divisions to withdraw." I held my breath and then said, "*Obergruppenführer*, the order from the Führer states quite clearly...".

A Tiger tank rolls forward as the German buildup for the titanic and decisive battle at Kursk begins (below). It would prove the greatest tank battle the world had yet seen. The new Tigers were complex and sophisticated in design.

A German crewman lies dead by the burning wreck of a panzer tank (left). The battle line-up shows the numerical superiority of the Russian forces (right).

BATTLE LINE-UP

GERMAN	SOVIET
men 900,000	men 1,300,000
tanks 2,700	tanks 3,600
guns 10,000	guns 20,000
aircraft 2,000	aircraft 2,400

'Paul Hausser interrupted me, "An old man like me is no loss, but I can't do this to the young boys out there. Give the corps the order."'

In the event, Hausser's withdrawal proved to be well judged – though it infuriated Hitler. It drew the Russians forward as they chased the retreating troops, leaving them exposed and eventually giving the Germans the chance to strike back. That they could even contemplate a counterattack was a remarkable testament to their fighting spirit. Since being driven from Stalingrad in February 1943, they had been driven back almost to the position they had started from a year before. All their efforts and casualties had been in vain.

The weary German troops had few illusions about the fate that awaited them. Soon they would face the massive resources of the Soviet Empire: And the mighty Russian armor, once called into battle, would be bound to triumph over the wasted panzers. But Hitler's orders were to hold on and press home the attack at any cost.

From late in 1942 to the middle of the following

War Stories

Lice plagued Russian partisans. Some engineers were enjoying a steam bath as their clothes were being disinfested when they heard an explosion. Rushing out naked to find out what was going on, they discovered that the detonation had been caused by the grenades and detonators they had left in their pockets, set off by the heat.

BATTLE DIARY
THE BIGGEST TANK BATTLE

DECEMBER 1942
16 Start of Soviet winter offensive
JANUARY 1943
12 Second phase of Soviet offensive begins and Germans retreat
FEBRUARY
2 Last German units in Stalingrad surrender
8 Russians liberate Kursk
16 Kharkov falls to the Russians
20 Manstein launches his counteroffensive
MARCH
15 Germans recapture Kharkov for last time
JULY
4/5 Beginning of German attacks on Kursk salient
12 Major tank battle around Prokhorovka
13 Hitler orders halt to attacks at Kursk
14 Red Army launches its counterattack
23 All German gains around Kursk recovered
AUGUST
23 Kharkov liberated for last time

Soviet troops on the offensive (left). Civilians return to the scenes of devastation at Kursk, after the town's liberation from the Germans on February 8 1943 (above); the Germans had destroyed anything of military use.

year, the Eastern Front battlefield moved to the steppes of southern Russia – vast, treeless plains which provided ideal terrain for tank fighting. Some of the Soviet Union's mightiest rivers – the Dnieper, Donets, Don and Volga – flow roughly north to south across the flat lands, forming virtually the only defensive positions in the otherwise featureless landscape, and fighting concentrated on control of the water barriers, the bridges which crossed them, and the railroad centers that served both troops and the Soviet industry based in the

Soviet crews proudly stand by their new T-34 tanks (center). A German assault gun is backed into a shelter (far left). A British swordsmith forges the Stalingrad Sword in 1943 (left); it was presented to Stalin by Churchill in honor of the Red Army's victories in their 1942/43 offensive.

A German, draped in camouflage, stands sentry over an antitank gun emplacement in the spring rains of April 1943 (left). Hundreds of dejected Russian POWs are led into captivity (bottom far right).

Donets basin.

Breaking out of Stalingrad, the Russians had advanced west to the towns of Rostov, Dnepropetrovsk, and Kharkov, from where Hausser was eventually forced to withdraw when 13 tank units threatened to overrun his defenses. The Russians pursued, overstretching themselves as the Germans had the year before.

Dozens of small German victories left the 4th and 1st panzer armies well positioned for a pincer attack against the Russians, aimed at driving them back across the Donets River. Army Group South, commanded by Field Marshal von Manstein, planned to attack the Russian left flank, recapture Kharkov, and link up with the 2nd Panzer Army to encircle the remaining Russian forces in the vicinity of the town

A MASTER OF TACTICS

Erich von Manstein was born in Berlin on November 24, 1887. He joined the Imperial Army in 1906, fighting with distinction in World War I. His natural aptitude and intelligence earned him promotion and in Russia, he was given command of the Eleventh Army. After Kursk, however, his open disagreements with Hitler finally led to his dismissal in March 1944. Nevertheless, he was generally considered one of the Nazis' best military tacticians.

of Kursk. Manstein's bold, ambitious plan impressed Hitler, when he visited the front on February 17, 1943, and blunted his anger at the loss of Kharkov.

The push began well. In the local area, Manstein enjoyed something like a seven to one advantage in tank numbers and three to one in aircraft, and swept the Russians back behind the Donets, recapturing Kharkov on March 15. In all, the Russians lost well over 1,200 tanks.

Once again the weather came to the Soviets' aid. The six-week spring thaw turned the steppes to a quagmire, preventing Manstein's plan from achieving total success. Nevertheless, he had managed to stabilize the front, and buy himself time to reequip his forces: They had dropped to only 140 serviceable tanks. But the Russians took advantage of the delay to improve their own resources. The ultimate consequence of the buildup of armor would be the greatest tank battle the world had ever seen.

The battle at Kursk on July 12, 1943, was the climax of the great German summer offensive, codenamed *Zitadelle*, or Citadel, which was designed to pinch off and destroy the

The citizens of Kursk begin the daunting task of rebuilding their shattered city following the retreat of the Germans (above). Soon they would be digging trenches for the elaborate defenses the Red Army constructed in the Kursk operation; Marshal Zhukov conscripted some 300,000 Kursk citizens to help.

Tiger tanks roll across the Russian plain (left). The German Ninth Army commander, General Model, discusses the advance (bottom left). The gun crew of a German howitzer duck for cover as a shell explodes nearby (bottom right).

Soviet armies caught in the so-called Kursk bulge, where they had moved forward too far ahead of their line, leaving themselves exposed on both flanks. Success would pave the way for further operations northward to isolate Moscow, and retrieve ground lost in the south since Stalingrad.

Among some German officers, however, great doubts persisted about the operation. It would lack any element of surprise, they argued: How could the Soviets fail to notice the massive buildup of forces? In fact, a spy-ring – known as the Lucy Ring – was passing secret German plans to the Soviets' military commanders.

THE PRODUCTION BATTLE

The 2,700 German armored vehicles at Kursk amounted to 61 percent of their total Eastern Front force, whereas the 3,600 Soviet vehicles comprised less than 40 percent of the Red Army forces. This was because the German tanks, such as the new Tigers and Panthers, were of such complex and high-tech designs that their factories could only produce the vehicles in limited numbers.

In addition, the launch of the operation was delayed, allowing the defenders of the Kursk bulge to prepare. Scheduled for May, Citadel was postponed several times – partly because there was a slight chance that further fighting could be avoided. Stalin was angry that the Western Allies had failed to open a second front in Europe to divert German troops from the east. Now he offered to make peace if the German army would withdraw to behind the frontiers that had applied in 1941. Talks began between low-ranking diplomats from both countries in June, but Hitler tried to impose conditions on

Reinforcements hurry forward as the Germans near Prokhorovka: T-34 tanks carry infantry to the front line, while overhead, dive-bombers race in for a strike (above). Marshal Zhukov (inset, right) took charge of the fighting here at its critical phase. Tiger tanks break through Red Army lines amid wasteland (right).

any deal that the Russian dictator could not accept. While the Germans delayed, the Russians waited, looking for an opportunity to resume the offensive. Forces within the bulge were reinforced to blunt the panzer assault and inflict heavy casualties in readiness for the counterstrike. Marshal Georgi Zhukov, who was in overall command, conscripted more than 300,000 local people from Kursk and other towns to begin preparing elaborate concentric fortifications. They dug more than 6,000

The insignia designating German antitank planes (left). German Stukas prepare to cause destruction (far left), while deadly Russian Katyusha rockets shoot skyward toward their target (inset left). German artillery closes in as Soviet T-34 tanks go on the offensive (bottom left).

A squadron of T-34s charges through one of the many gullies that cut through the plain around Kursk (right). A line of Soviet guns in action (below right).

THE LUCY RING

'Lucy' was the codename of Rudolf Rössler, an anti-Nazi exiled in Switzerland. With Hungarian and English accomplices, he supplied Stalin with detailed information on German plans, which he claimed came from some anti-Nazi officers in the German army. The ring was broken up when Germans discovered it and complained that it compromised Swiss neutrality, but its information was vital to preparing the defense of Kursk (*right*).

miles of trenches, laid minefields, dug in or camouflaged guns and tanks, and provided antiaircraft cover. Eventually, the Soviet forces around Kursk were stronger even than those which had defended Moscow.

When it finally came, the German attack got off to an inauspicious start: General Model's Ninth Army pushed forward in the north, as Manstein's South Army Group also advanced. But the Germans' plan had been revealed to the Russians by a Hungarian deserter.

Exactly 40 minutes before the German attack was

FATAL DELAY

The purpose of the German assault – to smooth out the Kursk bulge – was logical but poorly executed. The delay caused by Hitler's insistence on waiting for delivery of newly designed tanks, combined with the activities of the Lucy Ring, was fatal. By the time the panzers rolled forward on July 5, they encountered a 'brick wall': Stalin's forces had constructed one of the most elaborate defense systems of the war.

TURNING POINT

set to begin at 3:00 A.M. on July 5, Soviet artillery commenced a massive bombardment of shells raining down on the Ninth Army's start lines. Thrown into confusion, Model's forces were unable to move for 90 minutes after the planned time.

There was worse to come. Unable to make much headway under murderous crossfire, Model's force gained only six miles on the first day. Many of the units became bogged down in minefields, which had been laid with around 5,000 mines in every square

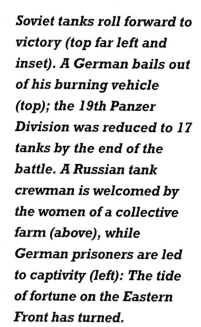

Soviet tanks roll forward to victory (top far left and inset). A German bails out of his burning vehicle (top); the 19th Panzer Division was reduced to 17 tanks by the end of the battle. A Russian tank crewman is welcomed by the women of a collective farm (above), while German prisoners are led to captivity (left): The tide of fortune on the Eastern Front has turned.

mile. The Soviet artillery and Katyusha rocket fire was deadly, and on the second day prevented the Germans gaining more than another four miles. On July 7, the attack was stopped in its tracks on the ridge in front of the town of Olkhovatka, and by July 12 Model had lost half of his tanks.

At first, Manstein's southern forces fared better, despite equally stiff resistance. Assault engineers went forward to clear a minefield southeast of Belgorod while the Luftwaffe kept the Russians' heads down. Only when the way was clear did the panzers clatter forward under the cover of darkness.

German infantrymen surge forward to storm a Russian post, July 5, 1943 (top), while grenadiers and SS men await their orders, sheltering in an antitank ditch made by the Russians (above).

The insignia of the 6th Panzer Division (above left). A column of German supply trucks and tanks, with troops on bicycles (above). Two Germans cautiously approach two wrecked T-34 tanks near an advanced German field position (right).

The insignia of the 3rd SS Division, Totenkopf, veterans of the Eastern Front (above left). German Panzer tanks advance across the vast and desolate plains of Russia (right). Although a tank bears the legend, 'We will conquer through Tiger' (left), this will not be the case at Kursk: Disaster looms for the Germans.

But daylight brought rain which slowed the advance, and the first Russian defense line the panzers encountered lay within heavily wooded country which proved difficult terrain for the tanks to negotiate. As a result, the Germans did not break through until the third day of the battle, July 8. The delay slowed the advance of Paul Hausser – who had so infuriated Hitler by abandoning Kharkov earlier in the campaign – whose rapid progress had to be halted while the flanking armies caught up. Eventually, German SS forces managed to cross the Psel River – the last defensive line before Kursk – and reached the village

Russian soldiers rest in a moment between attacks (top), while an antitank rifle crew dig themselves in and prepare for further bombardment at Kursk (above). Red Army antitank riflemen lie low and guard a hill (left). In the few hours leading up to the battle, more shells and bombs were used than in the whole of the French and Polish campaigns put together.

Russian artillerymen push their guns forward to fire at point-blank range at Kursk in July 1943 (right). Tense Russian antiaircraft gun crew fire at close support German aircraft (below right).

A former German strongpoint falls to Russian soldiers, August 1943 (below). The German invaders now face the full might of Russian resources; despite Hitler's orders to hold out at all costs, they have little hope of victory.

A despairing young German buries his head in his hands, his comrade dead behind him and his gun smashed beyond use (below). During the carnage at Kursk, more than two million men struggled in a battle which claimed countless lives.

of Krasny Oktyabr on the other side.

Now, as battle raged, the Soviet commander Vatutin deployed massive numbers of tanks in an effort to stop further German advances. On July 12, some 850 Russian tanks confronted approximately 700 German ones; despite the skill of the German crews they were seriously handicapped by being penned into an area only three miles square, as Vatutin had planned. The Russian T-34s charged forward and swarmed around the enemy, firing into the less well-armored flanks and rear of the German vehicles. The battle raged for eight hours, leaving orchards and cornfields blackened with fire and littered with the wrecks of tanks. Both sides lost about half their tanks, but the

loss was far more serious for the
Germans. The panzer forces
were left too weak to advance
further. Meanwhile, in the north, the German drive
had also been halted.

The Germans were spent, and the Soviet waiting
game could end. Their counteroffensive began
on August 3, when the Red Army advanced, tearing
open a 40-mile gap in the heart of Army Group
South. Sergeant Grigorii Sgibnev fought at Izyum, an
action for which he was made a Hero of the Soviet
Union.

'So long as we were running among the trees and
bushes, the Hitlerites remained quiet, but as soon as
we appeared in the open in front of the fascist
positions, their trenches became alive. Machine guns
and automatics rattled out. Grenades also flew to
meet us – one of them spun around beneath my feet.

'Everyone who has been in a battle knows the
feeling, when it seems that one is in the space
between life and death.... One acts automatically,
half consciously. I also, quite instinctively, seized this
grenade without thinking and hurled it back toward
the enemy trenches. It exploded as it reached them.
"Smash them with their own grenades!" I shouted.

*Defying orders to wait for
recovery vehicles, a
German Tiger pulls a
fellow tank out of a ditch
(above). Unless the
stranded tank could use its
engine to help, there was a
risk of damaging the other.
The insignia of the SS Das
Reich Division (inset).
General Paul Hausser, who
defied the Führer's order at
Kharkov (below).*

'Moving toward their trench, we bombarded it with the same grenades as the fascists hurled at us.

'I can remember I had managed to pull off the firing ring of one of my own grenades and was preparing to throw it, when a German grenade fell at my feet. I seized it with my left hand, and it exploded.... From hospital I went home. My father met me and said, "You've come back alive, that's the main thing".'

On August 11 the last battle of Kharkov began. Hitler gave another order to stand firm, but soon had to permit an evacuation. At dawn on August 23, the Red Flag flew again above the city center. In Moscow, Stalin ordered a 224-gun salute in honor of the victory: The once-invincible panzers had at last proved fallible.

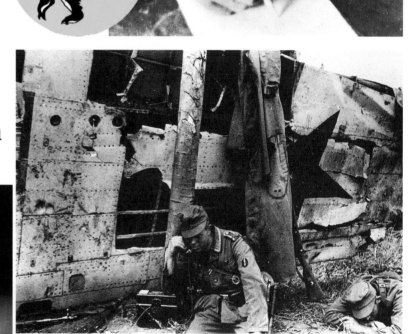

Major Hans-Ulrich Rudel, top antitank pilot (top). Hitler awarded him the Knight's Cross, and ordered him not to risk his life flying any more. Rudel said he could not accept the award if it meant being grounded. The insignia of the Panzer Bear Division (inset). A German field telephone operator shelters behind a wrecked plane wing (above). Tanks advance at Kursk (left).

In the Kursk bulge during an early morning attack, a German panzer explodes under a direct hit (right). Two Russian tank men examine a defunct Tiger tank (below).

Panzers press on through the rubble which is all that remains of a Russian village (bottom). Anticipating attack, Russian infantrymen wait in a trench in 1943 (far right).

JULY 1943-MAY 1944

The triumphant German advance into Russia had been overturned, and the once-proud soldiers now aimed only to return to their homeland. Still Hitler insisted that his dream of victory lay within reach.

By late 1943, with another cruel Russian winter approaching, the Red Army is well prepared against both the cold and the enemy (above). The wholehearted support of its war industry would keep it supplied throughout the freezing months.

Frost-bitten faces, stubbled chins, unbathed bodies: The weary German soldiers barely resembled the troops who had marched into Russia at the start of Operation Barbarossa two years earlier. Then they had been part of an irresistible force, renowned for its discipline and determination, and their minds were set only on their goal: The fall of Moscow. Now, in the wake of their defeat at Kursk,

their dreams of conquest were shattered. As Hitler insisted from the safety of Berlin that the offensive be renewed, and that indefensible positions be held at any cost, the frontline troops could spare no energy to think of anything but the needs of the moment: A drink, a smoke, some food or the merciful respite of sleep. For the rest of the war, most of them were to have no more ambition than simple survival as the enemy harried them back toward Germany.

Across a wintry wilderness stretching from the Baltic to the Black Sea, the Eastern Front had reached stalemate by late spring in 1943. Over the coming months, the Red Army would claw back the initiative and begin the drive to rid its soil of the Nazi threat. A series of mighty blows all along the front threw back the German invaders, never allowing them to regain their balance, as the Russians exploited the advantages of a huge pool of manpower and the factories which poured out munitions in the the Urals region.

The German retreat was sometimes orderly, and sometimes a headlong rush. The fleeing troops – harassed on every side by partisans, or guerrilla fighters – took vicious revenge on their tormentors

Léon Degrelle's Nazi insignia is admired by a group of young Belgian workers during a visit to Berlin (right). The commander of the Legion Wallonie, a force made up of pro-Nazi Belgians, Degrelle was to witness the full extent of the carnage as the Germans retreated. He inspired tremendous loyalty among his suffering men.

A Soviet aircraft production line (above). In factories throughout Russia, the people worked tirelessly for the war effort. After weeks of heavy fighting, the Russian army finally bridges the Dnieper River (right), breaching the most southerly point of Hitler's 'Eastern Rampart' before it had even been completed.

when they got the chance. They fired crops, burned bridges, razed entire villages and herded the civilian population and their livestock west in a policy known as 'scorched earth'. They left behind a barren wasteland where their Russian pursuers would find no food, shelter, fuel – nothing at all that could make their advance any easier.

The Soviet High Command, meanwhile,

MARSHAL IVAN KONIEV

Born in 1897, Ivan Koniev ranked second only to Zhukov as a Soviet commander. Koniev was one of the few officers to survive Stalin's purges of the 1930s. He combined with Zhukov in defending Moscow, and showed skill at Kursk, but it was his relentless hounding of Manstein in the Ukraine which earned him his reputation. He was made commander in chief of Soviet ground forces after the war, and later of all Warsaw Pact forces. He died in 1973.

Russian peasants who have seen their villages and crops destroyed proudly take up arms to fight and win back their homeland (below).

concentrated their efforts in the southern half of the front on clearing the Germans from the region of Ukraine – now an independent nation – bordering on the Black Sea. In a landscape consisting mainly of open plains or wooded lowlands, the chief natural obstacle facing the Soviet troops would be the Dnieper River which cuts across the heart of the region, averaging over 800 yards in width. They would have to force a passage across to succeed.

Realizing the obvious importance of the river, Hitler had ordered that it be heavily fortified: It formed the southern end of his so-called Eastern Rampart, a line of fortifications he hoped would give the Germans a defensible position. Both river banks were lined with barbed wire, minefields, concealed artillery and pillboxes. But before the Russians could attempt to breach the Dnieper Line, they first needed to clear the eastern Ukraine.

The new Soviet offensive began on August 26 and Manstein, commanding the German troops, had difficulty in

Russian soldiers, well insulated in winter combat dress, pick their way through the rubble that was once the town of Yukhnov (right). Buildings burn as the German army moves through the streets of Zhitomir (below).

preventing an orderly withdrawal turning into a rout. He described the war now as 'a defensive struggle which could not be more than a system of improvisations and stopgaps'. Before the Russian attack, Manstein had been reduced to fewer than 500 tanks and assault guns with which to hold a 1,300-mile front – about one every two-and-a-half miles. The Russians advanced so swiftly that encirclement was a constant worry. Nevertheless, Manstein's troops fought doggedly: The strategic town of Novgorod, for example, held out more than a week before surrendering on

Russian liberators tour Kiev, which was recaptured in November 1943. The burned-out shell of the city's university bears witness to the months of bitter fighting (below). The Soviets push the Eastern front further and further west as the liberation gathers momentum (below left).

BATTLE DIARY
RUSSIA LIBERATED

JULY 1943	**NOVEMBER**
13 Beginning of	6 Kiev recaptured
Orel offensive	**DECEMBER**
17 Beginning of	24 Start of Soviet
offensive against	winter offensive
Army Group A	**JANUARY 1944**
AUGUST	27 Official end of
3 Beginning of	siege of Leningrad
offensive against	**MARCH**
Army Group South	24 German troops
23 Kharkov	cross Dniester River
recaptured	**APRIL**
SEPTEMBER	10 Fall of Odessa
22 Soviet troops	**MAY**
reach the Dnieper	9 Final German
River	troops surrender in
25 Smolensk falls	Sevastopol

September 16. Only five days later, the first Soviet troops reached the eastern bank of the Dnieper north and south of the city of Kiev. Trofim Yaskil was one of the first men over the river:

'There had been no order from the regimental commander about the battalion crossing the river, but there was no time to waste. We had to force the crossing before the enemy had time to organize its defense.

'We rapidly crossed to the other side, taking with us a heavy machine gun, antitank rifles and antitank grenades. The enemy detachment did not put up much opposition to the incisive action of our troops, and fled in panic.'

Small bridgeheads were quickly established on the opposite bank, and by the end of September the

German position looked decidedly precarious: The 'Eastern Rampart' had been breached before it was even completed.

Meantime, further north, Army Group Center was facing a Soviet army group known as the Bryansk Front. German army commanders had decided to send five of the group's divisions south to help Manstein: Field Marshal Günther von Kluge was left with fewer than 300 tanks and assault guns. The result was inevitable. The Bryansk Front swept his forces aside. By the time the offensive ended in early October, von Kluge's men had been pushed back more than 150 miles.

Russian attention turned back again to the Dnieper bridgeheads in the south, through which they poured thousands of troops followed by hundreds of tanks. By mid-October Kiev, the Ukrainian capital standing on the river, was under siege; soon afterward Soviet troops struck south to seize the thin neck of the Crimea Peninsula on the Black Sea, trapping the German Seventh Army and cutting off all its supplies.

On November 3, the Red Army launched a final assault on Kiev with overwhelming numerical superiority. The 4th Panzer Army fought as well as it could, but the situation was hopeless; the city fell three days later. For a week more, the Red Army pushed on to the west. Then came a brief lull in the fighting: But the calm was deceptive. The coming Soviet storm would eventually drive Hitler's legions back behind their prewar frontiers.

The half-starved and exhausted German veterans had no illusions about what was coming. They had already endured two terrible Russian winter campaigns, and now they were locked into a third. But, before, they had been the agressors, with their sights set toward the east on Moscow, Leningrad, and Stalingrad. Now the tables had turned and it was their opponents who were striving for their own goals in the west: Budapest, Prague, Vienna, and, ultimately, Berlin itself. While the Russians were driven by the desire to clear their soil of the hated invader, the Germans had little strategy but simply to cling on to as much territory as they could.

The Soviet summer and fall offensives of 1943 had driven the Germans and their allies back beyond their 'Eastern Rampart' to the equally grandly titled 'Panther Line'. But such names were little more than figments of the Führer's imagination. To the weary troops at the front, they meant almost nothing.

The first blow of the Russian winter campaign fell on Christmas Eve 1943, when General Vatutin's First Ukrainian Front attacked Manstein's Army Group South. Despite being pushed back 125 miles in a week of furious fighting, the Germans succeeded in destroying or capturing more than 700 Soviet tanks and by the beginning of January 1944 had stabilized their line. But the Russians now held deeply

The shoulder badge of a junior lieutenant in the Red Army from 1943 (right).

The Russian army fights bravely in appalling conditions (left), as the spring thaw ends the bitter winter .

Red Army sappers, or engineers, cut through a barbed-wire fence to clear the way for the infantry's advance, in spite of nearby explosions (above).

Soviet troops battle for a railroad track (right) – one of many such struggles that add up to an advance .

General Vlasov inspects Russian soldiers who have surrendered and now fight for the Germans (below).

SHIFTING ALLIANCE

When the Germans invaded in 1941, much of the Russian population welcomed them as liberators. Thousands volunteered to fight with the Germans against communism. Many joined the Russian Liberation Army, formed by Lieutenant General Andrei Vlasov after his capture on the Leningrad Front in 1942. Vlasov's own division later turned against the Germans, but he was eventually executed for treason.

threatening positions in the rest of the Ukraine, and the situation was desperate. On January 4, Manstein flew back to Germany to try to persuade Hitler to pull back his whole southern flank. But Hitler refused to listen to his general, still trusting more in his overwhelming dream of defeating communism than in the practical advice of one of his best soldiers. He would not contemplate withdrawal. His unachievable dream would cost his troops dear.

At the turn of the year, 2.5 million soldiers in 185 Soviet divisions faced Army Group Center, which comprised around 600,000 German soldiers. A numerical superiority of four to one gave the Russians an unassailable advantage, and in fierce fighting the German Army Group was virtually

The shoulder board of a Red Army engineer lieutenant (above, right). The Belgian pro-Nazi leader, Léon Degrelle, commander of the anticommunist Wallonien Brigade, proudly sports the Iron Cross (above). The opposing forces for the battles in the Ukraine, 1944 (right).

BATTLE LINE-UP

German	Soviet
men 1,760,000	men 2,365,000
tanks 2,200	tanks 2,000
guns 16,000	guns 28,800
aircraft 1,460	aircraft 2,360

destroyed. For the young troops, the New Year of 1943 brought only horror. Only 23 years old, Lieutenant Erich Jainek found himself trying to evade capture with the remnants of his company, decimated by a Russian attack:

'In the course of a terrible, grinding, deadly odyssey, my company was ground down to only eight men. We waded through the deep snow at a fierce 40 degrees below, on field-compass reading 277 – directly west. We finally reached the advanced group of the 18th Panzer Division, drained, hungry and

War Stories

Aircraft 'nose-art' was not only practiced by US flyers. The Russians also liked decorating their craft – not with flashy pin-up girls, but in a quieter way. One pilot, a former Moscow Conservatoire student, spent many hours painting a musical score on his plane.

Soviet troops, apparently indifferent to the carnage around them, march into a recently recaptured Russian town (right). Young members of the German army march across the Russian plains into captivity, in the late spring of 1944 (below).

Retreat seems as tough as advance: A German pack mule column treks wearily westward through the forests of central Russia in the blizzards of January 1944 (right). By contrast, the Russians are now in their element. A group of guerillas discuss tactics for a raid against the Germans, who have little strategy left (below).

A Red Army tank captain's shoulder badge (left), and that marking a lieutenant in an artillery battery (far right). In the aftermath of another grim battle, German equipment lies abandoned (far right). Two winter campaigns have already been endured, and this, the third, is a massive challenge to both sides.

cold, at the end of a three-day march during which we had to fight the partisans.

'I was taken to the main field hospital on the back of a storm gun. There they discovered I had second or third-degree frostbite on both feet. It was only when I was at the hospital that I realized that I had marched about 80 miles to escape being taken prisoner by the Russians.'

On January 25, the Red Army launched

TURNING POINT

REVENGE

Once the Soviet juggernaut began to roll west after Kursk, little could stop it. With their numerical advantage, the Russians could attack in many areas at the same time. But they were also motivated by a burning desire for revenge against the Nazi occupiers who had brought such hardship and inflicted so much suffering, which spurred them on.

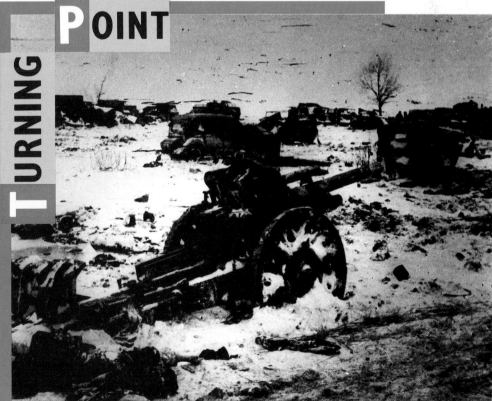

With little hope of long-term victory, two German grenadiers in winter uniform crouch in a gully, submachine guns at the ready, grimly awaiting Russian attack (below).

Bogged down in mud, a German ammunition column prepares to struggle on (right). As in previous Russian winters, the weather is a valuable weapon against the Germans.

a gigantic pincer attack which in only four days completely encircled two German corps in what was named the Cherkassy Pocket, after a town close by. The 56,000 trapped men – Germans, Belgians, Dutchmen, Danes, and Norwegians – fought back furiously, but the Russian commanders Koniev and Vatutin gradually tightened the noose.

Early in February came an unprecedented change in the weather, as temperatures soared and the thaw began. Trenches and bunkers were flooded with stinking mud and airfields became so waterlogged that it was impossible for the Luftwaffe to keep the trapped soldiers supplied. Léon Degrelle, commander of the Legion Wallonie, a brigade of Belgians who fought on the side of Hitler, was among those trapped in ever worsening conditions:

'Wherever we found ourselves, we soon came under enemy fire. Wherever we went we came upon dead horses, smashed-up vehicles, and corpses, which we no longer had time to bury.

'Since Tuesday morning it had been 20 degrees below freezing, and lying outside in their hundreds were wounded men whose faces were nothing more than a hideous violet mask, men with amputated arms and legs, dying men, their eyes rolling convulsively.

'Many of them had given up asking for help.... Every now and then the drivers would brush off the snow from these lifeless bodies with their hands. Many had been lying on these carts for ten days. They could feel themselves rotting alive. No injection could heal their most unbearable pains. There was nothing to be had. Nothing!

'The number of yellowing bodies beside the carts kept increasing. Nothing could surprise us any more, nothing could stir our feelings. When you've witnessed such horrors your senses are numb.'

General Wilhelm Stennermann begged Hitler to allow his forces to attempt a breakout, which began on February 16. All artillery had to be abandoned in the clinging mud and soft snow. The wounded who

A German grenadier, sheltered by his panzer tank, waits for a Stuka attack to come in and give overhead support (above). Fighting conditions are better in the early summer weather, as Germans fire at an approaching T-34 tank (below).

Mighty Russian rivers had often been an obstacle in the Red Army supply line, but by late 1943, the Dnieper was crossed by a massive pontoon bridge, carrying a constant stream of armor, food and ammunition much needed by the troops (right).

Red Army machine gunners of the 13th Guards Division await action on the banks of the river (left).

were unable to walk were also left to their fate, tended only by volunteer medics. After fierce fighting, in which General Stennermann himself died, some 32,000 men finally managed to escape.

As the saga at Cherkassy unfolded, Vatutin was busy in the north of the Ukraine, pushing the Germans back to within 18 miles of the pre-1939 border. The Russians were also making similar

headway in southern Ukraine and squeezing the Germans back toward the port of Sevastapol in the Crimea.

Nor were the Ukraine and Crimea the only targets for Russian attack at the beginning of 1944. Further to the north, where the German siege of Leningrad had lasted 30 months, Army Group North found itself facing the impossible disadvantage of an eight to one inferiority in tank numbers. Still, Germany's military planners insisted that the siege be maintained. Such an order was pure vanity, calculated to impress Hitler. In practical terms, it was suicide: The Germans lost two entire divisions as the Russians swept through the area, driving Army Group North south and west.

Back in the Ukraine, Manstein and Kleist were being forced back despite another of Hitler's orders to stand firm at all costs. By March 24, Soviet forces, now commanded by the wily Marshal Zhukov – Vatutin had been assassinated in February by pro-Nazi Ukrainian partisans – crossed the Dniester, the last river barrier before the Polish border.

Hitler had by now decided he had had enough of his commanders, and sacked them. After all that Manstein had achieved, his only reward was a handful of medals. Hitler had little more to show for the long

A train is destroyed at Belgorod after a major Soviet offensive. The invading Germans relaid tracks to run their own trains into Russia (right).

By the time Russia is able to reclaim the lands snatched by the invading Germans, her resources are so stretched that many of the soldiers are mere boys in their teens (left). German troops, meanwhile, have little choice but to carry on fighting to the end (below left).

A tense moment is captured on film as three Russian gunners stand poised to storm a German occupied building (right).

A group of Russian soldiers are pleased to find a huge collection of German military equipment (right). It has been left bogged down in the mud as the Germans retreat at long last. A group of German prisoners face defeat (below right). Some of them look strangely old and tough for boys so young – the war had made their growing up a very sudden process.

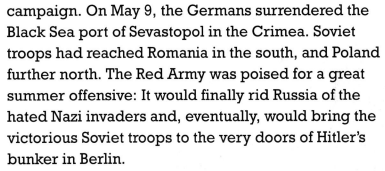

campaign. On May 9, the Germans surrendered the Black Sea port of Sevastopol in the Crimea. Soviet troops had reached Romania in the south, and Poland further north. The Red Army was poised for a great summer offensive: It would finally rid Russia of the hated Nazi invaders and, eventually, would bring the victorious Soviet troops to the very doors of Hitler's bunker in Berlin.

WARSAW

Three years after the German Army had launched Operation Barbarossa, Hitler's dream of conquest in the East lay in tatters. Some two million men had been lost. By the summer of 1944, the Red Army was rolling back the invader and in the process exacting a terrible revenge. Germany's time was coming to an end and much of Europe was about to come under the influence of new, Russian, masters.

A German half-track, fitted with metal framework 'cages' for field-rocket missiles, fires on a Polish stronghold in Warsaw during the uprising (below).

To the people of Poland's capital, Warsaw, the sound of artillery fire in the distance was a welcome one. For almost five years, the city had been occupied by the hated Nazis, and Polish resentment had reached breaking point. To the east, the Soviet Union was no friend of the Poles – the two countries had been at war little over 20 years before, and Stalin planned to control Poland when he had defeated

Hitler. But for now the muffled boom of the Red Army's guns as they approached the city could mean only one thing: Freedom from the Nazis. It could only be a matter of days before the Germans were forced to retreat from the city. On the afternoon of August 1, 1944, Warsaw erupted as Polish underground fighters rose to liberate their capital before the Soviets arrived. But the gunfire had been deceptive. No relief would come for the Poles for another two months. By then, the German occupiers of the city would have

A fairly well-equipped section of the makeshift Polish Home Army, or Armia Krajowa, some with wounds from recent action, stand on parade in Warsaw, August 1944 (below). They had developed into a formidable force, despite the years of occupation.

turned on its population with remarkable ferocity. The fighters of the Polish Home Army would be hunted down and driven into the sewers; those who helped them would be executed in the streets; civilians with no part in the fighting would be herded before German troops as they assaulted Polish positions. With the Russians held up outside the city, the makeshift army had little chance. The Warsaw Uprising was doomed to failure.

The Soviet summer offensive of 1944, codenamed Operation Bagration, had begun some six weeks

The armband of the Polish Home Army (above); one of its soldiers faces a German attack with just a rifle (right). By 1944 the army consisted of around 200,000 men and women, about a quarter of them in the capital.

earlier, on June 23, with a 1,800-gun bombardment on German lines, not in the Ukraine, where earlier fighting had been centered, and where the Germans expected the assault to come, but further north in Belorussia, which borders on the Baltic states in the northwest of the Soviet Union. The plan, named after one of the Russian generals who defeated the French emperor Napoleon in 1812, was timed to coincide with the Western Allied landings at Normandy, forcing Germany to fight on two fronts for the first time in World War II, and stretching the forces of the Third Reich to the limit.

Previously driven from their homes, Soviet citizens return to Vitebsk with their few belongings, after the city is liberated in June 1944 (above). In the same month, Soviet infantry advance toward Minsk, the main city of Belorussia (below). They are using an antitank gun for support.

The Germans were taken by surprise, and the Soviet superiority in arms and their better morale enabled their forces to gain quick victories over the weary Germans. Rapid encirclements and the overthrow of Nazi defensive strongholds netted thousands of prisoners before Soviet forces trapped some 100,000 Germans in Minsk, Belorussia's main city. By the time Minsk fell, on July 11, 70,000 of these defenders had perished; the rest surrendered.

When the victorious Russians entered the city, they found it in ruins. Even compared with the standards of their scorched-earth tactics elsewhere – in which

they left behind them a devastated land, destroying anything that might be of use to their Russian pursuers – the Germans in Belorussia had been particularly barbaric. Almost every public building in Minsk had been destroyed, and what remained of the population lived in hovels. Hundreds of thousands of civilians had been killed, and a similar number had been deported to work as slave laborers in Germany. In the countryside, the Nazis had not only burned the crops, but had used special deep plows on the land to prevent it being easily returned to cultivation.

With growing confidence, the Soviet forces pressed

War Stories

Young Poles risked being made to join the German labor force. The ID card of one guy who was stopped bore a grim-looking mug shot. 'You look just like the boxer, Schmelling. Do you box?' a soldier asked admiringly. 'I'll pretend I never saw you,' the soldier decided. The Pole's similarity to a childhood hero had saved him from a German camp.

Soviet soldiers replace a border sign, torn down in the attack three years before (above). Operation Bagration, the summer offensive, has finally driven the Germans from Russian

PARTISAN SUPPORT

In Belorussia there were an average of 1,000 sabotage incidents per month on the railroads by summer 1943. In some areas partisans held almost total control. Next year, the partisans went on the offensive. Supporting the activities of the Soviet air force, they set about blowing up bridges and railroad tracks and ambushing isolated convoys, hindering the movement of German reinforcements to the front.

on with a series of sweeping offensives which took them into Hungary and through the Balkans. By July 23, the Red Army had captured the Polish city of Lublin. Armored spearheads pushed ahead to the Vistula River, and established two bridgeheads on the far bank south of the Polish capital, Warsaw. But German resistance was stiffening, and the Soviet offenders were becoming exhausted by their rapid advance. On the banks of the Vistula, the Red Army ground to a temporary halt as it waited to resupply

BATTLE DIARY
BAGRATION AND WARSAW UPRISING

JUNE 1944
23 Operation Bagration commences
JULY
3 Minsk captured by Soviet troops
AUGUST
1 Warsaw uprising
8 German counteroffensive in Warsaw
20 Red Army opens offensive against German Army Group South, Ukraine
30 Polish Home Army withdraw from Warsaw Old Town

SEPTEMBER
14 Germans launch major attack in Warsaw
16 Renewed Soviet offensives against Riga and Tallinn on the Baltic coast
26 Polish Home Army's Mokotow garrison forced to withdraw
30 Germans capture Zoliborz in Warsaw
OCTOBER
2 Polish Home Army surrenders Warsaw to Germans and are treated as POWs

A Soviet senior lieutenant and an NCO discuss the next move forward as machine gunners fire with a 1910 wheeled gun (top right). Men of the 1st Front wade through a river on the road to Riga, July 1944 (above). The Soviet move to the Baltic encircled the remains of the once strong German Army Group North.

itself. For the citizens of Warsaw, it was a fateful delay.

Within the occupied city, the situation was tense, as an SS officer, Herbert Brunnegger, discovered: 'Warsaw was a dangerous place. Poland's capital was like a pot of bubbling lava whose lid was about to blow.

'It was strictly forbidden to go out alone or even in twos. If you wanted to go out in the city, you had to be armed.... Nevertheless, soldiers kept disappearing without trace. Their uniforms and weapons turned up again on men from the Polish underground.'

Warsaw had already been the scene of bitter fighting. Large numbers of Polish Jews from outlying areas had been herded into the city's tightly cordoned ghetto, where they had lived in terrible conditions. From July 1942, the Germans began their systematic deportation of the Warsaw Jews to the death camp of Treblinka. As the deportations continued, the Jews began to fight back, but could do little. What remained of the ghetto in Warsaw had been crushed in April 1943 by a ferocious onslaught

As Soviet infantry finally enter the Warsaw suburb of Praga (top), Operation Bagration has almost run out of steam.
A Soviet infantryman considers the damage done to a bridge over the Vistula River by the retreating Germans (right).

Polish Home Army officers – one wearing a captured German helmet – fire a heavy machine gun in the desperate struggle for Warsaw (left); a flamethrower team rushes forward, protected by riflemen (bottom).

of German artillery and tanks.

But there remained the Polish Home Army. The *Armia Krajowa*, or AK, had developed into a formidable fighting force, despite the years of German occupation. By 1944, it numbered around 200,000 men and women who maintained a campaign of harrying German garrison troops, keeping open routes for escaped prisoners of war, and running a

highly successful intelligence service which had, for instance, supplied the Allies with invaluable early warning of the German V-weapon – or rocket – program. The Home Army had a great weakness, however, in its limited supply of weapons and ammunition: It was estimated never to have possessed more than 32,000 weapons.

On August 1, 1944, the Home Army rose up against the Germans. The uprising was more than simply a military action: For the Home Army's masters in the

Buckets of petrol stand near a barricade in Warsaw, to be made into lethal Molotov cocktails by Home Army soldiers (left). A German officer orders his men forward to capture another Polish barricade (inset right).

Majestic Warsaw buildings blaze as citizens run for shelter, carrying a few precious belongings (right). The civilians have to endure a constant battering from Stuka and artillery fire. The relative losses suffered during the Warsaw uprising (below).

BATTLE LINE-UP

Home Army 40,000
Number killed 10,200
Number missing 7,000
Civilian population 1,000,000
Number killed 250,000

Men (12 August) 13,000
(after 20 August) 21,520
Men killed 10,000
Men missing 7,000

Life in occupied Europe was hell for Jews. One young Warsaw gentile was mistaken for a Jew and arrested. Like many others he protested his non-Jewishness, but unlike many he was set free. He had to prove that he had not been been circumcised by dropping his trousers.

Polish government-in-exile, based in London, it would also be a political gesture to show the world that Poland intended to reemerge as an independent state once the war was over. For history had taught the Poles to be fearful of their neighbors.

Poland had long been surrounded by powerful states – Germany, Russia and, until 1918, Austria-Hungary – all of whom had regularly carved up the

Warsaw citizens at a water rationing point, set up after the city's water supply system is badly damaged by bombardment (above). The dead often have to be buried in the streets (left). A captured German tank is used by the Polish Home Army, August 1944 (below).

country in the past. When Germany invaded Poland on September 1, 1939, the Nazis' aim was to destroy the Polish state once and for all – and in the Nazi-Soviet Pact the same year, Stalin had approved the plan and agreed with Hitler how the two powers would divide up their prize. By now, most Poles mistrusted and hated the Germans and the Russians in almost equal measure.

But the Nazi-Soviet pact had been blown apart by Hitler's invasion of Russia and now, as the Red Army rolled west, Poland's fate seemed to lie in the hands of Stalin alone. In London, the Polish government-in-exile found itself on the sidelines. The uprising was a

Exhausted and hungry, Warsaw citizens have to pay a heavy price for their support of the uprising: They face food shortages and constant bombardment (right). German soldiers are taken prisoner by the Polish Home Army (left).

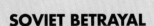

SOVIET BETRAYAL

TURNING POINT

Controversy will always surround the Polish decision to begin the Warsaw Uprising in August 1944. Did the Soviets deliberately abandon the Polish Home Army, allowing the Nazis to wipe out leaders who could have opposed a Communist takeover after the war, or had their offensive simply run out of steam? Both are probably true: It was probably a case of a practical problem being exploited for political gain.

Two days after the Polish surrender, men of the Home Army are still emerging from the maze of sewers which had been a means of survival (below).

last chance for the Polish people to have a say in their own future – and it was to fail.

In the summer of 1944, conditions seemed to favor the Poles' intentions. Lucjan Kindlein – who at the age of 21 abandoned his law studies to train with the military – shared the optimism of the young people who took part in the uprising: 'To a certain extent, we all enjoyed it, because it was the first time we could really stop running from the Germans – and make

them run instead.

'Street fighting is something you have to be specially trained for. We found that we could even cope with the tanks – and we didn't have to be afraid of them. In the town they were very vulnerable, and we threw grenades and burned them with gasoline.'

Although some of the older citizens of Warsaw were worried about what punishment an uprising might

The devastation of Warsaw (left). A nine-year-old boy has to wait three weeks in the sewers for treatment of his wounds (inset).

Civilians emerge from cellars and sewers in which they have sheltered and march to detention camps outside the city (below).

The streets of Warsaw are a battleground and its citizens struggle to continue their lives (below).

bring, most of the younger ones relished the opportunity, as Kindlein explains: 'The Polish Home Army was part of the overall operation of Polish forces. It was all geared to that final act – we wanted to show the Germans that we were in power in our country, and were taking revenge for what they were doing to us. It was also to protect our young people from being taken to labor camps.

'But the third and most important reason was that

Polish snipers pick their way through the wasteland (far right). Hitler's revenge against the Poles for challenging his power is harsh: Streets are reduced to rubble.

Warsaw, as a city in the center of Poland, had to be taken – not by Russians but by the Polish Home Army. That was why we had to do it.'

The Polish commander in chief, General Tadeusz Bor-Komorowski, had around 40,000 troops in Warsaw, with a further 11,000 in the vicinity of the city. But even though these numbers were larger than the German forces, Bor-Komorowski was hampered by an ammunition supply which ran to little more than a weeks' fighting; and he had nothing to counter the Germans' artillery, tanks, and aircraft.

The Poles' actual plan of attack was entrusted to the Commander of the Warsaw District, Colonel Monter, and it was he who led the Home Army in the ensuing weeks of combat.

From the afternoon of August 1, small-arm and

Herbert Brunnegger, a 22-year-old platoon leader in the SS Totenkopf Division, photographed just a few days after his return home to Germany (above right).

A very young recruit in a pitifully baggy uniform – one of the many young boys who did their bit to help in their war torn city (right). Some 200,000 of Warsaw's former citizens were buried beneath the rubble during the ruthless fighting of the uprising.

mortar fire could be heard all over Warsaw as an army of men and women in ill-assorted uniforms attacked German strategic centers. The Polish civilians were quick to welcome them. In the streets, people cried, 'At last! At last!', and women kissed their new saviors. The uprising had begun.

The German High Command was quick to react.

A group of young boys line up to carry the latest news of the uprising to other parts of the city. A number of broad sheet papers were produced underground during the German occupation (left).

The next day Hitler despatched a large contingent of crack SS troops – including renegade Russian forces and criminals released from German prisons – to do as much damage to the city as possible. From the air, the Luftwaffe bombed Warsaw at will.

During five days' fighting, the German garrison managed to hold onto key areas, effectively dividing Home Army territory into three separate and increasingly isolated sectors on which the Germans intended to concentrate their forces one at a time. They were a particularly ruthless enemy. As they fought their way through the streets, the Germans executed civilians and prisoners alike, set fire to hospitals with the patients inside, and drove civilians

A Polish underground soldier lays a charge to blow up a railroad line crucial for bringing in supplies to the Germans (above). Sabotage was an important part of the Warsaw people's opposition. Accustomed to the sight of dead bodies in the road, a German soldier continues down a muddy road (left).

in front of them when attacking Home Army positions.

In turn, Polish civilians rallied to give all possible help and support to their freedom fighters against the hated occupiers. At great risk, boy scouts and girl guides ran messages, and people willingly gave precious food to the Polish soldiers. The home of Marzenna Karczewska, who was only 19 when the uprising began, was used as a safe house for the Polish underground, so she was forbidden from getting involved in any military activity for fear of detection. Nevertheless, she helped support the Home Army: 'During the German occupation I was simply involved in preparing cigarettes for our soldiers who were in the hospitals. We'd make up parcels for them, or take them soup cooked in special field kitchens.

'Where there was fighting we helped, carried wounded, made bandages and did whatever was needed to help.'

On August 12, the German assault on the Old Town district began with a massive bombardment. Slowly

A POW ID card belonging to Marzenna Karczewska, who wears the uniform of the Polish 1st Armored Division – the group which liberated her POW camp (above). After the surrender, Warsaw women fearfully search notices on a fence for news of their loved ones (right).

but relentlessly, the Germans reduced the historic area to rubble with artillery, bombs, flamethrowers, rockets, and so-called 'Goliaths', remote-controlled

Bor-Koromowski surrendered on October 2, 1944: The uprising had failed. The people are still starving, and the Red Cross distribute precious bread to desperate Warsaw citizens (left)

Weary and gaunt, a Polish Home Army is interrogated by German officers after the surrender (right). The city would not be relieved, by Stalin's Red Army, until after the winter.

vehicles fitted with explosives. To keep communications going with the Home Army in the other areas of the city, Polish messengers were forced to crawl through the intricate sewer system.

On August 30, the sewers provided an escape route when Monter evacuated his troops from the Old Town to the City Center and Zoliborz districts. Marzenna Karczewska was among them: 'I was to go with my group – 39 of us – and we were almost the last group to leave through the sewer. It was very narrow – 30 by 31 inches. We had no idea what it would be like, but we tried to do it because we knew some people before us had.

'When we started the journey it was arranged that we'd go alternately, boy, girl, boy all the way down the line – but unfortunately the men were very weak. They were the worst, and they didn't have the guts to keep going. They got claustrophobia. They panicked and started shouting that they wanted to kill themselves – they said that they would be better off going and being taken by the Germans. We had to cover their mouths, we wanted to survive.' When the Germans overran the Old Town the next day, all they found was an empty, smoking ruin.

Meanwhile, outside the city, Soviet forces were mounting a concerted attack against German

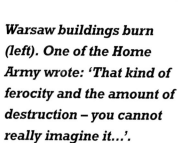

Warsaw buildings burn (left). One of the Home Army wrote: 'That kind of ferocity and the amount of destruction – you cannot really imagine it…'.

German soldiers take shelter (above). They were confident of victory in Warsaw, due to their vast superiority in resources and arms.

positions. Appeals to the West received sympathy, but there was little the Allies could do. Their bombers suffered heavy losses as they dropped supplies on the city with little success: On one mission, only 44 out of 149 canisters reached the Home Army.

On September 14 the Germans launched major

attacks against the remaining Home Army strongpoints. The Poles were at crisis point. Further attempts by the Red Army to cross the Vistula had been beaten back. The Home Army fought on as best it could.

By the end of September, only the Poles in the city center remained, their position hopeless. They had held out for 63 days when, on October 2, Bor-Komorowski surrendered. The uprising had failed. When the city was finally relieved on January 17, 1945, it was by Stalin's Red Army. As many Poles had feared, their long-awaited liberation only served to usher in a new era of domination, this time by the Soviet Union.

Lucjan Kindlein (above, right of picture, in helmet) was 21 years old when he left his law studies to join the military. He was proud to be part of the great national movement who would use all possible resources to reclaim their homeland and reassert their independence against Russia too.

INDEX

Numerals in italics indicate a photograph or illustration; bold numerals indicate volume numbers.

Acknowledgments

The publishers would like to thank the following organizations and individuals
for their contribution to this series:

Airborne Forces Museum; Associated Press/Topham; Australian Department of
Information; Australian Overseas Information Service; Chris Barker; Barnabys
Picture Library; Bill Bebbington; Bibliothek fur Zeitgeschichte; Bildarchiv
Preussischer Kulturbesitz; Major T. Bird; British Red Cross Archives/ICRC;
Vincent Brome; Herbert Brunnegger; Squadron Leader Bulloch; Bundesarchiv-
Koblenz; Henry Byrne; Camera Press; Robert Capa/Magnum; Cas Oorthuys
Archives; Collins Publishing Group; Colorsport; Alan Cooper; Giancarlo Costa;
Crown Copyright; Daily Telegraph/John Frost Newspapers; Dunn School of
Pathology, Oxford University; Far East War Collection; John Frost Collection;
John Frost Newspapers; Jim Goodson; Hulton Deutsch Collection; Zbigniew
Fleszar; E. W. W. Fowler; T & V Holt Collection; Robert Hunt Library; Hunting
Aerofilms; ILN Picture Library; Imperial War Museum; Jessop Classic Cameras,
London; Keystone Collection; Kobal Collection; Kodansha International; Kyodo
News Service; Andre Laubier; Hans Lemke; LFCDA; Librarie Academique
Perrin, Paris; London Transport Museum; Siegfried Melinkat; Moro Roma;
Munin Verlag GMBH, Osnabruck; Museum of Army Flying; National Film
Archives; National Museum of Photography, Film and TV; Peter Newark's
Historical Pictures; Peter Newark's Military Pictures; Peter Newark's Western
Americana; John Norton; Air Vice Marshall W.E. Oulton; Novosti Press Agency;
John Pimlott; Polish Institute/General Sikorski Museum, London; Polish
Underground Movement; Popperfoto; Bruce Quarrie; Queen Victoria Hospital;
RAF Museum, Hendon; James Ravilions; Rijksinstituut voor
Oorlogsdocumentatie; Ringier Dokumentationszentrum; George Rodger; Roger-
Viollet, Paris; Franklin D. Roosevelt Library; Royal Navy Submarine Museum;
Salamander Books; Science Museum, London; SCR Library
Mainichi Shimbun; Constance Babington Smith; Peter C. Smith; Alan Stripp;
Süddeutscher Verlag; Tass; The Tate Gallery, London; M. K. Tither; Carel
Toms Collection; Topham Picture Library; TRH Pictures; Ullstein Bilderdienst;
US Army; US Library of Congress; US Marine Corps; US National Archives; US
Navy; H. T. Wade; Arthur Ward Collection; John Watney Photo
Library/Interpress; J Wharton; Franco Zagari/F. Testi; Zeitgeschichte, Stuttgart

Front cover picture credits for the series:
Hulton Deutsch Collection, Roger-Viollet, Paris,
Popperfoto, US National Archives, Süddeutscher Verlag